100
DEVOTIONS
FOR PASTORS AND
CHURCH LEADERS

VOLUME 2

100 DEVOTIONS
FOR PASTORS AND CHURCH LEADERS

VOLUME 2

JOHN PHILLIPS

Kregel
Academic & Professional

100 Devotions for Pastors and Church Leaders, Volume 2

© 2008 by John Phillips

Published by Kregel Publications, a division of Kregel, Inc., P.O. Box 2607, Grand Rapids, MI 49501.

All rights reserved. Apart from the exception noted below, no part of this book may be reproduced, stored in a retrieval system, or transmitted in any form or by any means— electronic, mechanical, photocopy, recording, or otherwise— without written permission of the publisher, except for brief quotations in printed reviews.

Permission is granted to the user to reproduce not more than one devotion, or portion thereof, at a time in newsletters, Web postings, church bulletins, or other publications for not-for-profit use. A standard credit line must accompany any use, and include the title of this work, the author's name, the publisher, and the phrase, "Used by permission." Any other use of this material, except as allowed under copyright law, requires the prior permission of the publisher (rights@ kregel.com).

Scripture taken from the King James Version. Italics added by the author.

ISBN 978-0-8254-3388-7

Printed in the United States of America

08 09 10 11 12 / 5 4 3 2 1

I dedicate this book to Betty, for whom these studies were written. When I was courting her, Betty lived in California and I lived in North Carolina. Three thousand miles and three time zones stretched between us. As a result, much of our courting was done on the telephone. In time I ran out of things to say!

I decided to write her a devotional study every day. By the time I was finished I had written nearly three hundred devotions.

Here are one hundred of them, with Betty's earnest desire that they might be as great a blessing to you as they have been to her.

CONTENTS

Devotion I
SEPARATING THE WATERS

GENESIS 1

The works of God in creation, as recorded in Genesis I, illustrate the works of God in redemption. "Light be!" God said, and light was. It is a lesson in *salvation*. God begins by shedding light into sin-darkened souls. Darkness is dispelled. People see the truth. Their eyes are opened to see beauty in Christ. The power of darkness, including the power of spiritual darkness, is real enough; but it cannot triumph over light forever.

God's next movement in creation was to bring order out of chaos. He separated the waters from the waters. It is a lesson in *sanctification*. There came into being two vast seas, "the waters below" and "the waters above"; the sea, and that vast ocean suspended in space in the form of clouds. There are some 54 trillion, 460 billion tons of it, defying gravity and riding the hidden highways of the sky.

The waters below are virtually identical with the waters above. Both are made up of two parts of hydrogen and one part of oxygen. They are kept separate by means of an atmosphere. And their behavior is different.

The waters below always seek their lowest level. Their nature is to go down. Rivers have their origins high in the mountains, but they end up in the depths of the sea. The Amazon, for instance, has its source in the high wind-swept Andes of Peru closer to the Pacific than the Atlantic toward which it flows. Down it goes, thundering ever downward and gathering into its embrace other downward-flowing streams as it goes. By the time it reaches the ocean, it is a vast inland sea, with banks ninety miles apart, draining half a continent. Such, too, is the nature of humanity, born in sin. No person can lift himself back to the state of innocence that marked Adam and Eve before the fall. The second law of thermodynamics, which explains how everything is running down, from order to chaos, has its counterpart in the spiritual realm—in the "law of sin and death"!

The waters above, by contrast, represent those who have been redeemed. Clouds are comprised of water that has been brought under the influence and power of the sun. This water has been *changed* by evaporation. It rises to the heavens above and rides the currents of the air. In the form of a stream, transformed water can be *channeled* and put to work in the world.

These two oceans are separated by an atmosphere that the Bible calls *the firmament*. It is essentially "atmosphere" that distinguishes between unregenerate people and those who have been redeemed by Christ "the Sun of righteousness" (Mal. 4:2) and raised on high to sit with Him in heavenly places. The redeemed enjoy the atmosphere of the prayer meeting, the Bible class, the worship service. The lost seek the atmosphere of the ballroom, the tavern, and the theater. The atmosphere of the one is alien and foreign and unpleasant to the other.

Finally, God separated the sea from the land. The land was raised up from prairie to mountain peak. It is a lesson in *sovereignty*. In the symbolism of Scripture, the sea represents the nations of mankind, restless, storm-tossed, and troubled. The land symbolizes the nation of Israel, set in the midst of the nations and constantly attacked by their rulers but never subdued.

So creation points us to redemption and shows us God at work in salvation, sanctification, and sovereignty.

Devotion 2

LET THERE BE LIGHT

GENESIS 1:3–4

L ight be!" God said. "Light was," the Holy Spirit says. Just like that! Light is a mysterious thing. It travels at an astonishing 186,000 miles per second. In one second it can travel around the earth seven and a half times. Its speed is always constant. It never changes. The speed of light is at the heart of the famous equation that ushered in the nuclear age: $E = MC^2$ (energy equals mass multiplied by the speed of light squared). Light be! Light was!

It is not enough, however, to grasp the obvious, surface meaning of these words, that God brought light into being and chased away the darkness. God's Word is *God's* Word, so naturally it has depths upon depths to be explored. It is as fathomless as the being of God Himself. The Bible was not written to be a handbook of science, though whenever it has occasion to speak on a subject which falls within the domain of science it does so with infallible, inerrant accuracy. The Bible is a handbook of salvation. Things that we can learn by a process of human *reasoning* are left to us to discover for ourselves—the physics of light, for instance. Things we cannot know by mere reasoning are made known to us by a process of divine *revelation*. As truth is revealed by God in His Word, so light is shed abroad in our hearts and our understanding is opened to truth about which, before, we were in darkness.

Paul shows us how to look for deeper, spiritual truth beneath the surface of, for instance, a narrative portion of Scripture. He takes his illustration from our text here in Genesis 1:3–4. God said, "Light be," and light was. That is the obvious, outward, surface statement that barely needs comment. Paul ignores the physical aspect, the creation of light in the universe, and concentrates on the deeper, spiritual aspect. He says, "God, who commanded the light to shine out of darkness, hath shined in our hearts, to give the light of the knowledge of the glory of God in the face of Jesus Christ (2 Cor. 4:6). Beyond the creation story, Paul saw the redemption story. Doubtless there are even deeper depths to be discovered in the statement, "Light be, and light was." It will take us all eternity to explore all the unsuspected depths beneath the surface of God's Word.

It is John, however, who expounds the typology of light. He begins with *the light shining*. Jesus, he says, is "the true Light" (John 1:9). He well remembered Jesus' own words: "I am the light of the world" (8:12), and the sneering response of His foes. He is "the true Light, which lighteth every man that cometh into the world" (1:9). God sees to it that all people receive some measure of light. Jesus is the Light of the world.

Satan is the prince of darkness and wields enormous power. But he cannot stop the Light from shining. He tried it at Calvary, and failed. The darkness, John says, could not "comprehend" (*katalambano*) or *overcome* the Light (John 1:5). It never can. At Calvary the world did what it could to overcome and overpower the one who was the Light of the world. It failed. He, the Light of the world, was so completely in charge of things, that even while He hung upon the tree, He actually put out the sun and plunged the land into darkness for three interminable, terrifying hours. Just before He died He turned it on again (Matt. 27:45). The world thought it had put out the Light, once and for all, when Jesus' body was sealed in the tomb. Not a bit of it! He came marching back in triumph, holding aloft the very keys of death. Satan tries to put out the light of the gospel everywhere it shines. He cannot win (Matt. 16:18). Already the light shines around the world, and, in a day soon to come, it will dazzle every eye.

John tells us also of *the light showing*. Light exposes the hidden works of darkness. And "this is the condemnation, that light is come into the world, and men loved darkness rather than light" (John 3:19). Nowhere was this more evident than when the members of the Sanhedrin, instead of responding with joy and awe to the amazing news that Christ was alive from the dead, tried desperately instead to stifle it with lying propaganda and organized persecution of the church. They would not come to the Light, John said, lest their deeds should be exposed (3:20). For them, and their like, Jude says, "is reserved the blackness of darkness for ever" (v. 13).

"Light be," God says. "Light was," the Holy Spirit says. All those who open up their hearts to this light will find that "the path of the just is as the shining light, that shineth more and more unto the perfect day" (Prov. 4:18).

Devotion 3

NOAH WALKED WITH GOD

GENESIS 6:9

Noah walked with God." The Bible tells us so. It had been a long time since God had such a close companion on earth. The last man who walked with God had been Enoch, but he had been removed by rapture seventy years before Noah was born. Right after we are told that Enoch walked with God, we are told of the birth of Noah's sons. Noah was about five hundred years old when his firstborn, Japheth was born. So it had been a long time since God had been able to find a successor to Enoch.

The world was already a wicked place, and it went on becoming worse and worse until it was totally corrupt. Every imagination of the thoughts of men's hearts was only evil continually. Moreover, the world was filled with violence (Gen. 6:5).

But Noah "found grace in the eyes of the LORD" (Gen. 6:8). This leads us to think of Noah as *a person*. God said to Noah, "Thee have I seen righteous" (7:1). Noah was born in sin, just like everyone else, a child of Adam's fallen race. But there came a day when he was counted righteous by God (Rom. 4:3). Righteousness is not something we acquire by doing good; it is something imparted to us by God when we believe (v. 5). "Abraham believed God," we read, "and it was counted unto him for righteousness" (v. 3). Something similar took place in the experience of Noah, and God wrote it into his book: "Thee have I seen righteous." God had looked into the faces of millions of people. He had peered into their hearts, looking for a righteous man. He found only one. His name was Noah. The name means "rest." God found Noah to be a restful person. The name also suggests "comfort." Noah had about him the characteristics of the comforter. Such was Noah as a person.

We think, also, of Noah as *a preacher*. Noah is most famous, of course, because he built the ark, a place of refuge from the wrath to come. Peter reminds us, however, that Noah was also a preacher of righteousness (2 Peter 2:5). When Paul preached righteousness to Felix, that wicked man trembled (Acts 24:25). We read of no such reaction to Noah's preaching. The people had long since become gospel hardened. Noah preached for a *long* time, one hundred twenty years, without a single convert to add to the roll. There came a day, however, when he preached for the last time. Perhaps his last sermon was preached at the funeral of Methuselah, whose death rang out the knell of doom over that old and evil world. Methuselah's father was the prophet Enoch. He gave his son a prophetic name: "When he dies, it shall come" was what people said when they pronounced Methuselah's name.

Finally, we think of Noah as *a parent*. Noah had no success with this world's multitudes, but he had great success with his sons. He saw them all, along with their wives, safely inside the ark. Then the door was shut, and an eerie week passed during which nothing happened. But, at last, the first great drops fell from the sky, and the waters all over the world began to rise. The ark drifted away from its cradle and out upon the rising waves. A stab of lightning pierced the gloom. Noah counted up his passengers. All was well. At least his family had believed.

May our own circle be as unbroken as Noah's was in that day when God, once more, sends His wrath abroad. May all be in the Ark (Christ) saved from the judgment storm.

Devotion 4

TWO BIG DISAPPOINTMENTS

GENESIS 12:6, 10

He had become a pilgrim and a stranger in the world, in contrast with Cain who in his far-off day had become a fugitive and a vagabond on the earth.

His face was toward heaven, and his hope was in God. He was heaven-born and heaven-bound, and he looked for a city whose builder and maker is God. Abraham was his name. He was a Hebrew, a migrant, one who was just passing through.

But, on the way to his home up there, he was to inherit a land down here, a promised land. And into that land, the land of Canaan, he eventually came.

Imagine the shock and the dismay that were his when he discovered that there was a *foe*, the Canaanite, entrenched in the land. The Canaanites were a foul brood descended from Ham. They had a fierce and filthy faith. Imagine the further blow to his faith when Abraham discovered there was a *famine* in the land.

We know what he did. It is as plain as print on the page. He went down to Egypt and, in doing so, exchanged one set of problems for another. It was all so unnecessary, for all the time Abraham had with him all that he needed to deal with Canaanite and famine alike. He had a tent, and he had an altar. God's answer to the Canaanite was the altar; His answer to the famine was the tent. The altar was to teach him how to *die* to the Canaanite; the tent was to teach him how to *deal* with the famine.

The Canaanite represents the *flesh*. Often the young believer confidently expects, after his conversion, that all his problems are now solved. He expects to find nothing in his nature contrary to Christ. He is soon disappointed. The old nature is still there. More, it is awakened to active hostility to the new nature within. The believer finds he has begun what will be a war to the end. God's answer is the altar (a picture of the cross). It teaches us that "the old man," the person of old, the person we used to be (represented by the Canaanite) is crucified with Christ.

My father once asked Stephen Olford how he handled a believing brother who disliked him and sought to oppose him at every step. "Oh!" said young Olford, "I died to him years ago." Abraham had to learn to do the same so far as the Canaanite was concerned. So do we.

But not only was the Canaanite in the land, there was also a famine in the land. The famine in the Promised Land is a picture of the *world*, which can provide nothing to feed the spiritual nature of the believer in Christ. God's answer to the famine was a tent. Abraham lived in a tent, not a house. The tent was there to remind Abraham that he had already judged and forsaken this world. He was not to expect anything from this world, which is a barren place for the child of God. He was to strike his tent and move on as God led the way (Heb. 11:8–10, 15–16). He was to keep his eye on heaven, his final and eternal home. In the meantime he could well have sung:

> I am a stranger here,
> Within a foreign land;
> My home is far away,
> Upon a golden strand.[1]

In the end, after his disastrous Egyptian venture, Abraham had to come back to the place where his tent and altar had been at the beginning. That is how it always is for all those who have become pilgrims and strangers down here. They are citizens of a better land over there.

---

1. E. Taylor Cassel, "The King's Business," 1902.

Devotion 5

THE DEATH OF SARAH

GENESIS 23:1–19

Genesis is a book of funerals. The angel of death, the grim reaper, haunts it from beginning to end. The first death was a murder, but it also made a martyr. The last death was that of a rich and powerful man, dying in his bed, surrounded by his loved ones and placed in a coffin worth a king's ransom. But Joseph in his coffin was just as dead as poor Abel, whose stabbed and bludgeoned body was left to rot by the way to his house.

But of all the numerous deaths recorded in Genesis, there is none so sad as this one, sandwiched between a chapter that portrays the mystery of Christ's cross (Gen. 22) and a chapter that portrays the mystery of Christ's church (Gen. 24). The death of Sarah, between these two peaks, portrays the setting aside of Israel for this present age. Abraham, of course, could have known nothing of such truths, truths not to be revealed for another two thousand years.

We begin with *Abraham's grief*. His beloved Sarah was 127 years old (she is the only woman in the Bible whose age is recorded), but she looked more like twenty-seven. Kings had lusted after her beauty even in her old age. Her death left Abraham empty. Her name means "princess," and, like one born to rule, she was forever enthroned on the empire of Abraham's heart.

No longer would Sarah's bewitching smile bring sunshine to his soul. No longer would her imperious voice be heard in the servants' tents. No longer would she and Abraham sit together in the cool of the day talking together, praying together, content to be together. Abraham sat now alone in his princely tent, his thoughts full of that city "which hath foundations, whose builder and maker is God" (Heb. 11:10). That heavenly Jerusalem was doubly dear to him now for God, his Friend, was there and Sarah, his wife, was there. He wished that he, too, was there.

We think next of *Sarah's grave*. Her soul was in heaven, but her mortal clay needed a tomb so Abraham appealed to members of a nearby Canaanite clan, to the sons of Heth. Controlling his tears, he said, "I am a stranger and sojourner among you. Provide me a place for a tomb." Ever since Abraham's astounding victory over the kings of the east (Gen. 14), the people of Canaan prudently held him in awe. "Thou art a mighty prince among us," they said (Gen. 23:6). After this exchange of pleasantries, serious negotiations began. Abraham wanted a tomb; and Ephron, who had a suitable site for sale, wanted cold cash. No doubt Ephron set a ridiculously high price for the land as he expected Abraham to haggle, but price was no issue with Abraham. He was rich.

The story closes with *Ephron's gift*. When Abraham indicated what piece of property he desired, the sheik said, "I give it to you, my lord," but he would have been astonished and outraged if Abraham had taken him up on his words. That was but the opening gambit in an enjoyable bout of bargaining. "How much?" said Abraham. Ephron, expecting considerable hot debate, fixed the price at four hundred shekels and was doubtless astonished when Abraham paid him his price. The deed was "made sure" to Abraham (vv. 17–18). How sure? All we know is that Jacob had to pay for it again later on.

Such was Ephron's "gift." "Not as the world giveth, give I unto you," Jesus says to us (John 14:27). His promise *is* sure (Rom. 4:16), the Holy Spirit declares. How thankful we are that God's gift of eternal life is made sure in His son and that our title deeds to glory are as safe as God's throne.

JOSEPH AT HOME

GENESIS 30; 35:19; 37:11

Joseph had ten older brothers, one younger brother, and a sister. Since Jacob had four wives, all fiercely competitive to give him sons, his children were relatively close in age. Joseph lived in a disorderly home, for his father and mother doted on Joseph, and his older brothers detested him. Let us take a closer look at this home.

First, there was his mother, a very beautiful woman, and one who ruled supreme in Jacob's heart. Doubtless she shielded her beloved Joseph from the malice of his older brothers. She died, however, when Joseph was about seventeen years of age, and brokenhearted Joseph was thrown to the wolves. His father was in a fog of loneliness and unhappiness over the death of his dear Rachel and seemed unaware of Joseph's peril.

Then there was Joseph's aunt, Leah, a plain-faced woman. Jacob had never loved her with the passion with which he loved Rachel. In fact, she had married Jacob by being party to a trick promoted by her father, Laban. Many a time, likely enough, Joseph would find Leah crying in some remote corner of the farm. Never let yourself be used against your better judgment is the lesson of Leah. Never do someone a wrong just because that is the easy way out of a difficult situation. That was a lesson Joseph learned well and which stood him in good stead when he was confronted by Potiphar's wife.

And what about Grandpa Laban? What a fierce, grasping, unscrupulous, vindictive old man he was. Joseph saw clearly that Laban loved things and used people. Joseph learned from that. Joseph used things and loved people. Moreover, Laban was more than half a pagan. Watching Laban bow down to graven images taught Joseph the folly of idolatry—a valuable lesson when later he was brought into contact with the gross polytheism of Egypt, and was even married to the daughters of a pagan priest.

Joseph discovered what a bad lot some of his older brothers were. He was with the four slave-born sons of Bilhah and Zilpah. They were an unscrupulous quartet. Once out of sight of Jacob's encampment, they were up to all kinds of devilry. When Joseph refused to conform to their wicked ways, doubtless, they threatened him: "Don't you dare tell, you smug young psalm singer. We'll kill you." Joseph ignored their threats and told the truth about them. He learned thus how to take a lonely, unpopular stand for God no matter what.

His oldest brother, Reuben, was no help either. He had neither character nor courage. Joseph was doubtless aware of Reuben's adulterous affair with Bilhah, one of his father's wives. The sordid business, and Reuben's consequent lifelong fear of being found out, taught Joseph the high price of immorality. He vowed to steer clear of that kind of thing, at all costs. The price tag was too high.

As for Simeon and Levi, Joseph had good cause to fear the pair of them. Simeon was a cruel man, and Levi was even worse for he had a touch of the fanatic about him.

Then there was calculating Judah. "What's in it for me?" was his motto. He was the one who suggested selling Joseph into slavery for twenty silver pieces. No doubt he was motivated by the fear that Jacob would give the double portion of the birthright blessing to Joseph. Judah would have had designs on that for himself.

And what about Dinah, Joseph's only sister? Well, she was seduced as a result of some clandestine trips to the nearby town of Schechem and by the friendships she forged with the unsaved. Terrible, indeed, were the consequences. Joseph learned the lesson well—playday is followed by payday.

But the dominating member of the family, when all was said and done, was Jacob. Joseph was into his teens, and old enough to learn the value of a new life in Christ, when Jacob came to the Jabbok and was changed from Jacob to Israel. All these things molded and made Joseph, as God knew they would. That is why He put Joseph in that family. He has equally good reasons for putting us in ours.

Devotion 7

GO TELL MY FATHER

GENESIS 45:13

The scales had fallen from their eyes, and they knew him at last. "I am Joseph," he said (Gen. 45:3). "Ye sold. . . . God did send" (vv. 4–5). Then came the challenge. "Tell my father of all my glory in Egypt, and of all that ye have seen" (v. 13). That is the very essence of worship, to tell the Father of the beauty of Jesus that we have seen. This challenge was twofold. First, it required the brothers to *expose their sin.*

The last time they spoke to their father about Joseph was when they brought home Joseph's coat of many colors, all stained with blood. They had thrown it at Jacob's feet and (disowning Joseph) demanded: "Do you know whether or not this is your son's coat?" Now they have to confess. We can well imagine the things they had to say.

"Father, we have seen him, your son. He is alive! We have seen his glory! We hated him, father.

"We hated him for *the life that he lived,* a life so different from ours. He always did those things that pleased the father, and we hated him. He showed us up.

"We hated him for *the truth that he taught,* especially for those dreams of his that spoke of his exaltation and glory. He declared that every knee would bow to him one day. We hated him.

"We hated him for *the witness he was.* He brought to you the evil report of our ways. And we were wicked, father. He simply bore faithful witness to what he heard and saw. We hated him.

"We hated him for *the authority he assumed.* He was your well-beloved son, and he wore that royal robe you gave him like a born prince. He exercised the authority it bestowed, the authority you gave him. We hated him.

"We envied him. We could not speak peaceably to him. He came to us, and we received him not. We sold him for the price of a slave and handed him over to the Gentiles." *That* was how they must have begun—with *the exposure of their sin*.

But, then, this confession required them to *exalt the Savior*: "Tell my father of all my glory . . . that ye have seen," Joseph said. They would continue: "Now, father, our eyes have been opened. We see him now, at last, as you have always seen him.

"We have seen *the glory of his person*. We only saw him before as one of us, engaged in the everyday affairs of life. But now, ah, now! We have seen him enthroned in splendor surrounded by magnificence beyond anything our imaginations could have conceived. We have been awed by his wisdom, his love, and his power. And we have been made the recipients of his grace.

"We have seen *the glory of his position*. All we have ever known is a beduin camp; but now, down here in Egypt, we have seen another world, a world the like of which we never dreamed could be, a world of towering pyramids, a world where gold is as common as brass, where power is godlike, and where runs a river that brings life to all. We have seen the high throne on which he sits, and we have seen his great and gifted servants rushing to do his will. And now he has a name above every name, and before that name every knee must bow.

"We have seen, too, *the glory of his power*. He wields absolute power, but he wields it in benevolence and for the blessing of all.

"Finally, father, we have seen *the glory of his pardon*. He did not, for one moment, excuse our sin; but he covered it with his grace. It was all overruled by God, he said, so that he could become the savior of the world.

"But that is not all. He has arranged that where he is, there we shall be, also."

"Tell my father of all my glory . . . that ye have seen," said Joseph to his brothers. "*Go tell My father of all my glory that ye have seen*," says the Lord Jesus to us.

Devotion 8

THE PASSOVER

EXODUS 12

T he circumstances were *dire* enough. The Hebrews were prisoners in Egypt, held in a ghetto in Goshen. The king's command was still in force—wipe out the Jews. There could be no hope of escape, not so long as Pharaoh's soldiers guarded the ghetto. As for the Promised Land, all hope of that was just about gone.

The kinsman-redeemer had come, but nothing had changed. Egypt had been leveled to the dust by plague after plague, but the pharaoh was still on the throne. He remained unbroken, unbowed, unbelieving, determined not to let his captive Hebrews go. Such were the circumstances. They were dire enough.

And the solution was *drastic* enough. God's avenging angel would smite all the firstborn of Egypt. God would give them a holocaust. It would put such fear of God in Pharaoh's heart that, out of sheer terror, he would finally let the Hebrew captives go. The avenging angel of death would be sent forth by God to smite and kill every firstborn of man and beast throughout the length and breadth of the land.

But what about the Hebrews? Hebrew homes were in Goshen, and Goshen was part of Egypt, and all Egypt was under the interdict of God. Something would have to be done. But what? God gave His people a conditional guarantee from death.

The guarantee was *distinct* enough. A lamb must be taken, a lamb without blemish or spot. It must be slain. Its blood must be applied to the lintels and doorposts of each individual home. The avenging angel would *pass over* every house so marked, and the blood of the slain lambs would speak for the people of God. So the Hebrews remained in their blood-sealed homes, feasted on their Passover lambs, and made ready for the march.

Now let us look at Moses. He brought *the message*: "When I see the blood, I will pass over you" (Exod. 12:13). A great deal of truth was intertwined with the death of the Passover Lamb. From *a* lamb it became *the* Lamb (pointing directly to Christ) and finally *your* lamb, injecting the personal note. A house could be too little for a lamb, but the Lamb was never too little for the house.

Then, too, the Passover was a milestone. With Abel, it was a lamb for the *individual*. With Abraham, it was a lamb for the *family*. Now it is a lamb for the *nation*. At Calvary, it would be a lamb for the *world*. So Moses brought the message: "When I see *the blood*." The avenging angel, however, would not be deterred by a bucket of blood on the doorstep. It had to be applied. Paint on the doorposts would not do. There was no cheap way to secure redemption. A sign, "Moses lives here," for instance, nailed to the door, would not do. Moses was a younger son, so he was safe. But he had an elder brother, Aaron. Aaron wasn't safe. And Moses had an eldest son, Gershom. Gershom was in peril until the blood was applied. Once the blood had been applied, however, all was well. At peace with God and sheltered by the blood, Moses could feast and face the triumphant future God had planned.

To some, perhaps, even in Israel, the message of an avenging angel and salvation by blood must have seemed nonsense, repulsive even, the message of a madman. If there were such skeptics in the camp that night, and if they followed the dictates of their human reason, scorning divine revelation, they found out too late their mistake.

There was the message. It was followed by *the miracle*. Who but God could have known, in each and every house, who the firstborns were, or have selected, in every barn and field, the firstborn of every cow or sheep or dog or cat? It was uncanny. It was unerring. It was God. And all of it, pointing with steady finger down the unborn ages to Jesus, the true Passover Lamb, who paid for our redemption with His blood.

Devotion 9

THE HOLY OINTMENT
Part 1

EXODUS 30:22–33

There was nothing like it in this world. It was prepared from a special formula revealed to Moses by divine inspiration of the Holy Spirit. We are told *how it was produced*—five hundred shekels of this, two hundred fifty shekels of that, a little of this and some of that, no more, no less. The ingredients, spices drawn from here and there, were rare and costly and were mixed with a lavish hand.

The shekel used for weighing these costly spices, worth a king's ransom, was the shekel of the sanctuary. Among the Jews the ephah was used for dry measure, the cubit was used for lineal measure, the hin was used for liquid measure, and the shekel was used for measuring weight.

The shekel of the sanctuary, the sacred shekel, was heavier than the ordinary shekel. God expects more from us, when he weighs us, than we expect of ourselves. In ourselves we are all like poor, lost Belshazzar—weighed in the balances and found wanting (Dan. 5). We can persuade ourselves that we have performed in a satisfactory way, but our scales are inaccurate. So much of our performance is made up of personal ambition, pride, love of position, love of praise, and such like things. God sifts all that out when He weighs us.

It was by the high and unerring standard, the shekel of the sanctuary, that God weighed Christ. "I am well pleased," He said (Matt. 3:17). We can be sure God used no lightweight measure in passing verdict on Him.

Five hundred shekels. Think of it! Half a shekel was the ransom price for an Israelite under the Law (Exod. 30:11–16). When numbered, each man had to bring *half* a silver shekel—the price of his redemption. A *full* shekel tells us that the ransom has not only been paid, but fully and adequately paid. *Five hundred* shekels implies a measure of redemption only God can comprehend. *Five hundred plus* two hundred fifty plus two hundred fifty plus another five hundred tells of a redemption beyond all human thought.

We are told *why it was provided*: to anoint the tabernacle, and the ark, and the table, and the candlestick, and the altar of incense, and the altar of burnt offering, and the laver (Exod. 30:26–28). In the outer court, *where grace was shown*; in the Holy Place, *where God was served*; in the Holiest of all, *where glory was seen*; all was made fragrant by the anointing. God wants the fragrance of Christ to be everywhere—*everywhere!* Aaron and his sons were to be anointed and also prophets and kings. All who serve the Lord must carry with them the fragrance of Christ, whose very name "is as ointment poured forth" (Song 1:3).

Finally, we are told *how it was protected*. It was not to be copied. "Whosoever compoundeth any like it, or whosoever putteth any of it upon a stranger, shall even be cut off from his people" (Exod. 30:33). Christ did not come so that we might imitate Him, but so that we may be indwelt by Him. He who gave His life for us now gives His life to us so that everywhere we go we might carry with us His fragrance. May we do just that!

THE HOLY OINTMENT

Part 2

EXODUS 30:22–33

It was unique. The Jews were forbidden to make its like. It was to
be neither imitated nor profaned. Its ingredients and their amounts
are given. It all speaks of Christ. First, we have the *myrrh*. It points to
the *passion* of Christ. Myrrh was a resinous gum derived from a tree of
the terebinth family. It grows in the dry desert wastes of Arabia. The
myrrh, used in making the anointing oil, is described as "pure" myrrh.
The Hebrew word for "pure" is said to describe the swallow, darting
in the sky. The Lord Jesus, in His life, was as free as the birds of the
air. Christ's death was voluntary. His death was like the free-flowing
myrrh. Myrrh was obtained by incisions made in the tree. It was used at
weddings and funerals. It added fragrance to life's gladdest and saddest
hours. Five hundred shekels by weight was the contribution of the myrrh
to the anointing oil. That amounted to one third of the total weight of
the whole. The same is true of the four Gospels also. The heavy emphasis, in all of them, is the death of Christ. John's gospel, for instance,
devotes about half of its space to the events of the last week of our Lord,
to the events, that is, connected with His death.

The next two ingredients were *sweet cinnamon* and *sweet calamus*. They
point to the *Person* of Christ. It took two ingredients to depict the Person
of Christ because Christ united two natures in His being, the human and
divine. He was both God and man. Cinnamon comes from an evergreen
tree of the laurel family. The inner bark yields a light brown spice. In olden
times it was more valuable than gold. The Lord in His Person was like
that—an evergreen! He was the "blessed man" of the first psalm. "His
leaf also shall not wither," the psalmist said (v. 3). He was the God-man of
Philippians 2:5–11. Death itself could not overcome Him. When the time
came, He laid down His life Himself. He dismissed His Spirit Himself.

The calamus was a reed, pointing to the sky, a species of tall grass—depicting the fragrant humanity of Christ. He grew up as a tender plant, rooted to earth but pointing to the sky. The plant had to be crushed before its full fragrance could be obtained. The holy anointing oil called for two hundred fifty shekels of cinnamon and the same amount of calamus. The deity and humanity were perfectly balanced in the Person of Christ.

The *cassia* points to the *perfection* of Christ. It belonged to the same family as the cinnamon. A full five hundred shekel measure of cassia was required. The cassia reminds us of the Lord Jesus as He is presented in the typology of Scripture. The prophetic Psalm 45 said of Him: "All thy garments smell of . . . cassia" (v. 8). This plant grows where others die. It was used to blend all the other ingredients of the holy ointment. Oh, the pungency of the holiness and perfection of Christ. Bullying Pilate himself was overwhelmed by it. It threw wicked Herod into sharp reaction and open ridicule. It was strong enough to conquer the grave.

But the ointment, with all its pungent ingredients, needed one more thing—*oil*. The oil points to the *position* of Christ as the Anointed One. The oil speaks of the Holy Spirit. The oil took all these various fragrant excellences of the Lord Jesus (symbolized by the myrrh, the cinnamon, the calamus, and the cassia) and blended them together. It was the Holy Spirit who took the various excellences of Christ—His passion, His Person (both human and divine), His perfection—and transformed them from a collection of superlatives into one glorious, breathtaking whole and blended them into one inimitable fragrance.

One of the Lord's most eloquent titles was "the Christ," the Anointed One. He is God's anointed Priest. He ministers thus in heaven, filling that glorious place with the pervading fragrance of His presence. He is God's anointed Prophet. Truly, no man spoke like this man. And He is God's anointed King, coming soon to restore Edenic conditions to this world.

In the meantime, He anoints His own. Nobody was allowed to imitate that ointment, but God was willing to share it with us. Nobody can imitate the life of Christ. But we may have His fragrance shed abroad in our hearts by the Holy Spirit.

Devotion II

THE INCENSE

Exodus 30:34–38

The incense was burned on the golden altar in the Holy Place of the temple. On the Day of Atonement it was carried in a golden censer into the immediate presence of God in the Holy of Holies just beyond the temple veil. It had four ingredients. They were blended together in the order in which they are listed—stacte, onycha, galbanum, and frankincense. Incense is a symbol of prayer, ascending to God in a fragrant cloud from the golden altar. It is hard for us to pray, so the Holy Spirit helps us and even makes intercession for us (Rom. 8:26–27). His instructions regarding the incense are a step in this direction.

The *stacte* suggests *patience* in prayer. The Greek word *stacte* translates a Hebrew word that literally means "to drop" or "to distill." The thought seems to be "to distill as the dew." Dew is distilled secretly, in stillness and in silence. It takes time for dew to form. That is the first ingredient of prayer—patience. We must take time to pray. We must be still.

The *onycha* suggests *penitence* in prayer. The Hebrew word is thought to refer to a perfumed mollusk, which had to be crushed to yield its fragrance. This suggests to us that we should be crushed by the enormity of our sins. We might well be overwhelmed by our sins, by their constant repetition and by their continuing reign. Repentance is what we need, penitence in prayer.

The *galbanum* suggests *praise* in prayer. The word comes from a root meaning "to be fat, or fertile," possibly referring to the sap—the life, strength, and virility of the tree, the pith and heart of the plant. Galbanum added strength and vitality to the other ingredients of the holy incense. It is the rising sap that brings out the leaves and the flower and the fruit of the plant. It is praise that brings life into our prayers. Praise is the most important part of prayer, closely akin to worship.

The *frankincense* suggests *petition* in prayer. Frankincense is mentioned repeatedly in the Bible. It was one of the things the wise men brought to the infant Jesus. The word comes from a root meaning "to be white." It comes from the same root as the word "Lebanon"—"the white mountain," referring to the snow that crowns the mountain range's brow. If there is one thing that must mark our petitions, it is purity. God says if we regard iniquity in our hearts, the Lord will not hear us (Ps. 66:18). We ask and receive not because we ask amiss to consume it on our lusts (James 4:3).

The gum from which frankincense was derived comes from a plant in which the number five predominates. It bears five petals and ten stamens. The fruit is five-sided, and there are five species of the plant. In Scripture the number five is associated with grace. The frankincense reminds us that our prayer ascends to the throne of grace (Heb. 4:16). Incidentally, frankincense comes from a tree that grows on bare, inhospitable rock. This reminds us that prayer draws its strength from Christ, the Rock of Ages.

There was one other ingredient in the incense—salt ("salted" is translated "tempered together" in the KJV). Salt suggests *pungency* in prayer. How dull prayer meetings often become! If our *speech* is to be seasoned with salt (Col. 4:6), how much more our prayers! Surely we should give as much attention to making our prayers interesting as we do to making our conversation interesting. It is bad enough to be a bore in general speech. It is well nigh criminal to bore people with our uninspired, insipid, repetitious prayers. Surely it is time we came with the disciples of the Lord Jesus and say to Him, "Lord, teach us to pray."

Devotion 12

THE COLT

The lowly donkey is mentioned more than a hundred forty times in Scripture. The first mention is in connection with Abraham who, when told by God to go to Mount Moriah and there offer up his well-beloved son, immediately saddled his beast and prepared for the journey. Then there was the Good Samaritan's donkey, and what about Balaam's donkey, which rebuked the madness of the prophet? But surely the donkey that heads the list is the one mentioned in the Gospels, the one that helped the Lord Jesus fulfill an ancient prophecy (Zech. 9:9).

There are three things worth noting about this donkey. First, *it had to be redeemed*. The Law of Moses pronounced the donkey an unclean animal. It did not chew the cud, and it did not have a cloven hoof; so it was doubly cursed. Inside and out, it was declared to be unclean; and the Law demanded that any firstborn donkey should be put to death. But the Law also made provision for the condemned beast to be redeemed. A lamb could die in its stead. It could live because a substitute had taken its place and died.

The application is to us. We are born unclean, condemned by God's law, and sentenced to death. A Lamb (the Lord Jesus) has died so that we might go free. For, like that donkey of old, we needed to be redeemed. How grateful we should be to the Lord of glory, who took our place and died that we might live. Truly we now live the life of another, even of Him who interposed His precious blood and paid our debt and gave us His life.

But this colt needed not only to be redeemed, but also *it had to be released*. "Ye shall find a colt tied, whereon yet never man sat," Jesus told His disciples. "Loose him, and bring him hither" (Luke 19:30). It had life, thanks to the lamb, but it did not have liberty. That colt may have stood alongside the post to which it was tied and dreamed about being set free. The grass on the hills looked so green. The brook down the hill looked so refreshing. The other animals seemed to be roaming at will. But he was tied to a post. It was set free by the word of Christ and by means of His authority.

Again, the application is to us. Many have new life in Christ but are still in bondage to old habits and sins. They need to hear the Word of the Lord: "Loose him! Bring him to Me." How grateful that little colt must have been when the Lord's disciples undid the knots that bound him to that post. He kicked up his heels. He was free.

But there was something else. *It had to be ruled.* This was a colt upon which "yet never man set." It was an unbroken colt, full of the pride of life and self-will. But the Lord had not set it free to please itself but to serve Him. "Bring him to Me," He said.

Then a wonderful thing happened. The Master enthroned Himself upon the colt as Lord of its life. All rebellion fled. All fear vanished. The colt was transformed from a wild, untamed creature into an obedient, submissive instrument of the Master's will. Its one duty now was to lift up the Lord Jesus. And so it did. As a result the people saw Christ and shouted His praise. All eyes were on Jesus, not on the donkey; and that, of course, is the way it ought to be.

> How I praise Thee, precious Savior,
> That Thy love laid hold of me;
> Thou hast saved and cleansed and filled me
> That I might Thy channel be.[1]

---

1. Mary E. Maxwell, "Channels Only," 1900.

Devotion 13

THE FEASTS

Passover, Unleavened Bread, and Firstfruits

LEVITICUS 23

The Old Testament called for the annual celebration of seven man-datory and meaningful feasts. These feasts were separated into two groups. Four of them took place at the commencement of the religious year. Then came a pause, after which the three remaining feasts were kept. These feasts are prophetic in character. The first four feasts antici-pated Christ's *first* coming; the last three anticipated Christ's *second* com-ing. The two-thousand-year period (so far) covered by the church age separates the two comings.

We shall begin with the *commencement feasts*, the first four feasts that were fulfilled at Christ's first coming. Three of these anticipate the work of the *Savior*. The remaining one anticipates the work of the Spirit.

The Feast of *Passover* points to our *redemption*. On the tenth day of the month the people took a lamb free from all blemish and kept it tethered until the fourteenth day. During this period it was closely watched. It was killed on the fourteenth day between the sixth hour and the ninth hour. On the original Passover, the night of the Exodus, its blood was applied to the lintels and doorposts of homes so that those sheltering behind it would be saved from the avenging angel's sword.

The Feast of *Unleavened Bread* (which lasted a week) was closely associ-ated with Passover. The Passover lamb was killed on the fourteenth day. Immediately afterward, on the fifteenth day, a weeklong feast, known as the Feast of Unleavened Bread, began. The Hebrews were to thoroughly cleanse their houses of all leaven. Leaven in Scripture is used by the Holy Spirit as a type of sin. The Feast of Unleavened Bread points to our *regeneration*. The old is purged out, and the new takes it place.

Two of the feasts lasted a week; the others were one-day affairs. The feasts that occupy a single day point to some specific act of God—

Passover, for example, takes us straight to Calvary. Feasts that lasted seven or eight days (Unleavened Bread and Tabernacles) point to future events destined to span well-defined periods of time, namely the church age and the millennial age.

Note God's order with the Feast of Unleavened Bread. First, the blood was applied. Then came feasting on the lamb. Only then was leaven put out of the house. That is God's order. First there has to be redemption. Then a clean lifestyle must follow. God's house is prepared as God's home. The Hebrew housewife was diligent in her search for lurking leaven. She scoured every cupboard, every nook and cranny of the house, to make sure that not so much as a scrap of leaven remained.

In the New Testament leaven is a picture of hidden sin. Leaven in a loaf of bread, for instance, speaks of those things which, once introduced, continue to work away in secret until their activity is killed by fire. Throughout the whole period of seven days, vigilance had to be maintained lest leaven be somehow introduced. During this church age in which we live, constant watch must be maintained so that no corrupting influence lurks in our homes and no hidden sin is allowed to remain unjudged in our hearts.

The Feast of *Firstfruits* points to our *resurrection*. This feast was kept on the first day of the week, on the Sunday after Passover. This was the very day Christ arose from the dead. The farmer cut one golden sheaf from the harvest field and brought it to the priest, who waved it before the Lord. It foreshadowed the full harvest soon to come. The Feast of Firstfruits was fulfilled when the Lord was raised from the dead and when many other dead people arose at the same time, went into Jerusalem, and appeared unto many (Matt. 27:52–53). These people correspond to the wave sheaf. In His resurrection and in their resurrection, we see the sure promise and guarantee of our resurrection. All these things the Savior accomplished for us at His first coming. He has *saved* us, *sanctified* us, and *secured* us. We can rest assured as to that.

THE FEASTS

Pentecost

LEVITICUS 23

The seven Old Testament feasts were divided into two sections. The first four commenced the series and had reference to events connected with the first coming of Christ. Of these, three direct our attention to the work of the Savior. The fourth, the Feast of *Pentecost*, directs our attention to the work of the *Spirit*.

The word *Pentecost* comes to us from the Greek. It is the Greek word for fifty. Because it was fifty days from the Feast of Firstfruits to Pentecost, this feast is sometimes called "the Feast of Weeks." There were seven full weeks to which was added another day. Thus the Feast of Firstfruits and the Feast of Pentecost were celebrated on the first day of the week. These Old Testament feasts anticipated the end of the Jewish Sabbath and a new emphasis on the first day of the week as a day of rest and rejoicing.

"When the day of Pentecost was fully come," says Luke in recording the momentous events in the upper room (Acts 2:1). The feast had come and gone for some fifteen hundred years; now it had fully come. As all the typology connected with it was fulfilled, the Old Testament shadows gave way to the New Testament substance. The Holy Spirit came in a new and living way. Judaism was replaced by the church. The annual ritual, with its burnt offerings, with its sin offering and peace offering, and with its two loaves, was swept aside. A new day had dawned.

On the Day of Pentecost a hundred twenty individual believers in Christ assembled in the upper room, a room full of memories for the disciples. The church was born in that room with the sound of a mighty, rushing wind and amid a blaze of cloven tongues of fire. In that room the Holy Spirit baptized a hundred twenty separate believers into one body, "one loaf." As the wind drives away the chaff, so that mighty, rushing Pentecostal wind swept away the past that was centered in a now dead Judaism. The cloven tongues of fire symbolized the new cleansing and irresistible power now inherent in the church, the mystical body of Christ. The loaf represents the one body, in contrast to the multiple grains of corn on the wave sheaf. Over a hundred individual believers went into the upper room. One body, one church, came out.

The Old Testament ritual, however, actually called for two loaves, not just one. That was because Pentecost took place in two stages. Only Jews were present in the upper room on the Day of Pentecost in Acts 2. Later on, in the house of the Roman centurion Cornelius, Gentiles were added to the church. The same apostle was the chosen agent of the Holy Spirit on both occasions. The same phenomenon of tongues was present both times—the first time to convince the mass of unbelieving Jews in Jerusalem, the second time to convince the skeptical Jewish members of the church. There were two loaves—but there was only "one bread, and one body" (I Cor. 10:17). Gentiles did not have to become Jews in order to become Christians. Jews and Gentiles were impartially baptized by the Spirit into the same mystical body of Christ. The middle wall of partition between Jews and Gentiles was swept away (Eph. 2:13–16; 4:4–6). Before long, Gentiles would become a permanent and overwhelming majority in the church. Note that there was *leaven* in the two loaves. This was because the loaves represent the church, which has never been wholly free from sin.

The process begun at Pentecost goes on, for the Holy Spirit continues to add new members to the mystical body of Christ. Thankfully it will continue till Christ comes again.

Devotion 15

THE FEASTS

Trumpets, Atonement, Tabernacles

LEVITICUS 23

The first four feasts all pointed to the first coming of the Lord Jesus. They had to do with the *commencement* of God's personal invasion of *history*, the *work of the Savior* in terms of redemption, regeneration, and resurrection, and also the work of the Spirit.

Then came a pause of length. The feasts of the commencement period were counted by *days*. The Passover was killed on the fourteenth day. Unleavened Bread began the next day. On the morrow after the next Sabbath, Firstfruits was celebrated. Fifty days were counted from then to Pentecost, which foreshadowed the *work of the Spirit*.

But there was no counting of days to the next feast (Trumpets). We are simply told it fell on the seventh month. This time lapse foreshadowed the time from Pentecost to the rapture of the church. We do not know the precise time covered by this period, but the Feast of Trumpets looked ahead to future events connected with the nation of Israel.

Thus we come to the *completion* feasts, Trumpets, Atonement, and Tabernacles. Just as the first four feasts all anticipated the first coming of Christ, so the last three feasts all look ahead to the second coming of Christ. Just as the first four feasts were all fulfilled to the letter, and to the day, at the Lord's first coming, so the last three feasts also will be fulfilled to the letter and to the day. We can be sure of that.

The Feast of *Trumpets* focuses on the *gathering*. Trumpets figured prominently in Israel's national life. Two silver trumpets were made from the redemption money given by the Hebrews for the building of the tabernacle. They were sounded when the tribes were called upon to march, when it was necessary to sound an alarm because danger threatened, and when all the assembly was required to appear before the Lord. The prophet Isaiah tells how "the great trumpet" will regather the scattered

Jewish people in the end times (27:13). The first beginning of this return has already begun. Already Jews back in the Promised Land number several million. During the period covered by the Apocalypse, trumpets will herald certain events—in particular seven trumpets will sound as the Antichrist comes and furthers his nefarious plans (Rev. 8–9).

The Feast of *Atonement* focuses on the *grief*. In reality this feast was a fast, a time of national conviction and repentance. It was the day when the sins of the nation were covered up for another year. It anticipates the day when the Jewish remnant, in the end times, will see the returning Christ and will be convicted because of their age-long rejection of Him.

The Feast of *Tabernacles* focuses on the *glory*. It was celebrated after the harvest was gathered in (Deut. 16:13). It was a weeklong festival of praise and joy. It anticipates the millennial reign of Christ. An extra day (an eighth day) was added. In Scripture the number eight is associated with resurrection and a new beginning. The music scale illustrates this. There are eight notes in the scale, but the eighth note is the same as the first one, only it is an octave higher.

The millennium will end in judgment; but that will not be the final end, for God will begin again, but on a higher note. He will create a new heaven and a new earth and usher in an endless, eternal day of bliss and joy.

These things told in Old Testament typology in the annual Jewish feasts will as surely come to pass as did the things that pertained to the Lord's first coming. Any day now, the trumpet will sound. The church will be gone, and Israel will enter into its time of trial and ultimate blessing.

Devotion 16

TEN SHEKELS AND A SUIT

JUDGES 17–18

Judas sold Jesus for thirty pieces of silver. Jonathan, the grandson of Moses, sold his soul for ten shekels and a suit. The introduction of apostasy into Israel was *an infamous thing*. It all began in a small way. A man named Micah stole 1,100 shekels of silver from his mother. Frightened by her curses, he confessed and restored the money. His mother took 200 shekels and had them made into idols, and Micah put them in a shrine.

About this time, a wandering Levite from Bethlehem showed up. Micah saw an opportunity to legitimize his false religion. He propositioned the Levite. "Come and dwell with me," he said. "I will promote you from being a mere Levite to being my priest. I will feed you, and I will give you ten shekels of silver and a suit." The Levite's name was Jonathan (Judg. 18:30). His father was Gershom, the son of Moses (I Chron. 23:15). He was a contemporary of Phinehas, the grandson of Aaron, who is mentioned in his capacity of high priest as making inquiry before the Lord at a time of national crisis.

Thus early did apostasy rear its head in Israel. It seems incredible that Moses' own grandson should be at the heart of this infamous thing. Once Micah had installed Jonathan as priest of his new religion, he felt he had legitimized it: "Now know I that the Lord will do me good, seeing I have a Levite to [be] my priest," he said (Judg. 17:13). He and his hired Levite had forgotten the second commandment: "Thou shalt not make unto thee any graven image, or any likeness of any thing that is in heaven above, or that is in the earth beneath, or that is in the water under the earth. Thou shalt not bow down thyself to them, nor serve them: for I the LORD thy God am a jealous God, visiting the iniquity of the fathers upon the children unto the third and fourth generation of them that hate me; And shewing mercy unto thousands of them that love me, and keep my commandments" (Exod. 20:4–6).

Thus idolatry took root. It was an infamous thing. It was also *an infectious thing*. It started as a family affair but soon became a tribal affair. The tribe of Dan still had not settled in the territory assigned to it by God. It so happened that a band of landless Danites came across Jonathan, the Judean Levite. It seems that they knew him, and they were curious about his new occupation and intrigued by his reply. The six hundred armed Danites were swift to make up their minds. "Forget this fellow, Micah," they said. "Come with us. We'll make you priest to a whole *tribe*. Go and get the fellow's gods." The apostate Levite, a grandson of Moses, called of God to defend the Mosaic Law, was delighted. "The priest's heart was glad," the Holy Spirit says (Judg. 18:20). His fortune was made! And his judgment was sure.

Thus idolatry proved itself an infectious thing. The Danites "set them up Micah's graven image, which he made, all the time that the house of God was in Shiloh" (v. 31).

Ten shekels and a suit! How cheaply an apostate Levite sold his soul and seemingly prospered. Soon the infection of apostasy spread to the whole nation of Israel. The days of the Judges saw the virus incubate and spread. It was cleared up by David, but broke out again under Solomon, and in the end it doomed the monarchy. It all began with ten shekels and a shirt.

Now then, Jonathan, go and explain yourself to Moses and to God on the judgment side of death.

ELIMELECH

Moving to Moab

RUTH 1:1−5

The events recorded in the book of Ruth seem to have taken place early in the days of the Judges, at a time when the Promised Land was at rest. God's displeasure with His people was evident just the same, being expressed by means of natural phenomena, such as the famine mentioned in the book. They had not yet been sold into bondage to the surrounding foes.

The story revolves around four people: Elimelech, Naomi, Boaz, and Ruth. We begin with *Elimelech* and his family. First, we see them *moving to Moab*. It was a disastrous move.

In the Old Testament all God's promises and blessings for His people were centered in a *place*; in the New Testament they are centered in a *person*. In the Old Testament one had to be in *Canaan*; in the New Testament one has to be in *Christ*. It was in the Promised Land that God met with His people. It was there He put His name. It was there He made good His promises and centered His purposes. It was a disastrous decision, therefore, for Elimelech to move to Moab—even more so since Moab was a land under the curse of God (Deut. 23:3). To move to Moab meant leaving the fellowship of God's people. It meant removing the family from every means of grace associated with the company and gathering of God's people, feeble though they seemed to be.

Elimelech's name means "My God is King." That was all well and good, but he denied the sovereignty of God in his life when he decided to move to Moab. Doubtless, he had plenty of excuses. "There was a famine in the Promised Land," he no doubt said. There were job opportunities in Moab. He did not intend to stay in Moab. He would be back when things improved. All the usual things people say to encourage themselves in pursuing a wrong path were likely said by Elimelech.

Next, we have *marriage in Moab*. Instead of growing to manhood surrounded by young Hebrew women, Elimelech's boys had only pagan girls from whom to choose a partner for life. Their in-laws were raw heathen, and their chief god was the diabolical and bloodthirsty Chemosh, the devourer of little children. It was just as well that both Elimelech's sons were sickly and that they had no children of their own. Moses would have been against marriage with Moabites (Deut 7:3) or any other kind of marriage with unbelievers.

But then comes *misery in Moab*. Elimelech died. Then his two sickly boys died; and Naomi, now a bitter, old woman, "was left" (Ruth 1:5). That's how the Holy Spirit puts it—left, stranded in a foreign country with a couple of unsaved, widowed daughters-in-law. The breadwinners were gone. Naomi was out of the will of God, far from the place where God met with His people, and she was surrounded by pagans in a heathen land. Such was the end of Elimelech's backsliding. He lost his life in Moab, and he lost his family in Moab. The cost of backsliding is high. His good intentions of returning to the Promised Land never materialized.

Moab is an expensive place to raise a family. Those who leave the house of God and wander off into the world stand the risk of losing their children. Elimelech and his sons died in Moab, far from the fellowship of the people of God. How solemn, and how sad! The New Testament makes it a doctrine: "Be ye not unequally yoked together with unbelievers: for what fellowship hath righteousness with unrighteousness? and what communion hath light with darkness? And what concord hath Christ with Belial? or what part hath he that believeth with an infidel? And what agreement hath the temple of God with idols? for ye are the temple of the living God" (2 Cor. 6:14–16).

ORPAH FALLS FROM GRACE

RUTH 1:11–15

Orpah turned back, and it was impossible to renew her again unto repentance. God blots her name out of His book, and we read of her no more. Her story revolves around three choices.

Her first choice was to marry into a family of believers. She came to know the family very well. Perhaps often around the family supper table she would hear Elimelech and Naomi talk nostalgically about the true and living God, how He had sent them a kinsman-redeemer to deliver them from bondage and death. He had put them under the blood, He had brought them through the water, and He had gathered them around the table. He had given them His laws and had given them their land. She listened to their Bible stories, fascinating and factual stories about Adam and Eve, Enoch and Noah, Abraham, Isaac, and Jacob. She heard about God's wisdom, love, and power. But, alas for Orpah, she was wedded to her idols. Truth penetrated her mind but never touched her heart.

So Orpah made her first choice. She married into a family that had personal knowledge of God. Before her lay the opportunity of coming to know that God for herself.

Then came *her further choice.* Sorrow came into her life. Death came calling again and again until Naomi, Ruth, and Orpah all became widows. Then Naomi decided she'd had enough. News that God had been visiting His people back there in Bethlehem helped her make her decision. She would return to her people and her God. That was when Orpah made her second choice. She would go with Naomi. Naomi's God would become her God, and Naomi's people would become her people. Ruth made the same decision. So far, so good. But everything would hinge on what happened next. The three widows said their last, sad farewells at the graves of their departed loved ones and set their faces toward the Promised Land.

But now comes the tragedy in Orpah's life—*her final choice*. She began to lag behind. Naomi's warning about there being little or no hope of remarriage among the Hebrews took over her mind. Perhaps it would be best to go back to Moab. At least she might find a Moabite husband; after all, she *was* a Moabite. She came to a stop, and the other two came back to her; but Orpah had made up her mind. She would go back to *her* people and her gods. And so she did. The call of the true God faded away in her soul. She went back to seek rest with a Moabite husband.

Let us suppose that, still young and attractive, she married a Moabite man. Let us suppose, too, she did find rest in his house. What kind of rest would it be? At best it could be just *temporal* rest—a measure of peace and quiet, a share of this world's goods, enjoyment of this world's pleasures and pastimes, attendance at the more pacific and harmless rituals at the local temples and shrines—followed by a Christless death.

But there was a darker side to pagan religion, one that Orpah seems to have forgotten. Perhaps Orpah gave birth to a girl, a pretty girl with the earthly promise of beauty of face and form. The priests of Baal might mark her for the temple, to become a harlot, consecrated to the foul Moabite gods and to be debauched by priests and people alike. And Orpah's rest was gone forever.

Or, perhaps, Orpah gave birth to a boy. The priest of Chemosh might cast his evil eye on her little boy and put a mark on him. "Bring him to me at the temple tomorrow," he might say. "We'll find a place for him on Chemosh's lap. You are a woman favored of the god." What then of Orpah's rest? Gone! Forever gone. It was a terrible choice she made—to settle for the world's uneasy peace.

Devotion 19

ELI

Eli was Israel's high priest in the closing days of the judges, a time when immorality and apostasy went hand in hand. He was Israel's high priest, but he really had no claim to the position at all. He was not descended from the family of Eleazar, to whom the high priesthood belonged, but from the family of Ithamar, Aaron's youngest son. It is typical of the confusion of the time that we have no idea how he came to be high priest. It is typical, also, that his whole career (as recorded in I Samuel) was one of utter failure.

First, he was a failure as a *person*. He was old. Young men see visions, the Bible says, and old men dream dreams. Eli dreamed away his days. "His eyes were dim," the Holy Spirit adds (I Sam. 4:15). He was physically blind in his old age but also blind to the needs of the people. "Where there is no vision, the people perish" the Scripture declares (Prov. 29:18). Poor old Eli was blind even to the state of his own family. Typical, too, was his treatment of Hannah. He could not even tell the difference between a drunken woman and a devout worshiper, and he had some harsh words for that brokenhearted soul. His half apology, when he realized his mistake, does him no credit either (I Sam. 1:13–17).

So, there was Eli, old, slothful, worn out, content to sit in his rocking chair and doze away his days while Israel sank ever deeper into the mire.

Then, too, he was a failure as a *parent*. "His sons," we are told, "made themselves vile" (3:13). Their behavior was a national scandal. It was not safe for an attractive woman to bring a sacrifice to the altar. She was likely to fall foul of the lawless lusts of Eli's sons. When people complained, Eli shrugged his shoulders and went back to sleep.

Eli's sons also sinned against God. The Levitical Law set aside a portion of each sacrifice for the officiating priest. The fat, however, was to be burned on the altar. That was God's portion. Eli's unscrupulous sons dared to rob God. They appropriated the fat for themselves (2:12–17). Eli merely slapped their wrists. He should have thrust them out of the priestly office. Instead, he indulged them.

Doubtless, he had never curbed them, never taken the rod to them, to break their wills when they were young. They grew up willful and wild, and wicked beyond words. So Eli's failure as a parent was a serious thing, for he contributed two unregenerate sons to the priesthood. It brought about the downfall of his house.

Finally, and worst of all, Eli was a failure as a *priest*. He seems to have had little or nothing to do. He stands in contrast with Samuel, who went up and down the land seeking to arouse an apostate and apathetic people to a sense of sin and need. Eli waited for people to come to him. Few came. So all we see is a tired old man dozing in the sun.

The *first* time we meet him in the Bible he is propped up against a post of the tabernacle idling his life away. Later we see him sound asleep in bed. A little lad, entrusted to his care, had to wake him up three times before it finally dawned on him that God had something to say to the boy. Eli had long since ceased expecting that God might have something to say to him. The *last* time we see him he is sitting on a chair by the roadside. He fell off that seat and broke his neck. Such was Eli.

But there was one bright spot. He did a good job of bringing up little Samuel. Or did he? Maybe it was not so much due to old Eli that Samuel turned out so well. Perhaps that was a result of his mother's earnest prayers.

Devotion 20

AHITHOPHEL
David's Judas

2 SAMUEL 15:12, 31; 17:23

God forgave David, both for the seduction of Bathsheba and for the slaughter of Uriah. God forgave him, but Ahithophel never did. Ahithophel died by his own hand, cursing David, but with crimes on his conscience far exceeding anything David had on his. He died on a gallows in Giloh. He died nursing a malice and hatred for David that beggars description. And thereon hangs a tale.

We are prone to think of David as a type of Christ, and rightly so, for he was a type of Christ in many ways, especially in his early years when he was "a man after God's own heart." But there was another side to David, as there is with all of us. And it is this other side that is brought so sharply into focus in his contacts with Ahithophel. There are three aspects to the story.

We begin with *David's friend*. In one of his great psalms, David describes Ahithophel as "mine own familiar friend, in whom I trusted, which did eat of my bread" (Ps. 41:9). In another psalm he calls him "a man mine equal, my guide, and mine acquaintance. We took sweet counsel together and walked unto the house of God in company" (Ps. 55:13–14). It was no accident that David chose this man to be his primary counselor, for Ahithopel had a great deal to contribute to David. He was the cleverest man in the country; and, at times, his advice was little short of inspired. Moreover, he was not only David's counselor, but he was also David's companion. They would walk together to the house of God. He was also David's confidant. David would share his secret dreams and desires with him, his plans for the future of the kingdom.

But then, Ahithophel became *David's foe*, his bitterest, most malignant and formidable foe. Absalom's rebellion would never have got off the ground had not Ahithophel gone over to Absalom's side. Ahithopel had two main objectives in mind when he went over to Absalom. He wanted David's wives, those left behind in Jerusalem, to be publicly seduced by Absalom on the rooftop of the palace, before the public gaze (2 Sam. 16:20–23). His goal was to make sure that the alienation between David and Absalom was beyond reconciliation. His second, if not his primary goal, was to kill David. When David was in full flight from Jerusalem, Ahithophel pleaded with Absalom to let him take a band of soldiers on a swift expedition to corner and kill David before David could organize his own forces (17:1–3). Such was the fierce hatred that now burned in the heart of Ahithophel toward the man to whom he had once professed love and loyalty.

But why the change? The answer lies in *David's folly*. It was folly for David to loll around the palace when his soldiers were off to war. It was folly for David, when he caught a glimpse of Bathsheba in her bathrobe, to venture a second look. It was folly for him to seek an introduction to the woman and to cultivate the acquaintance, especially when he discovered she was married, and married, no less, to Uriah, one of his personal bodyguards. It was folly supreme to seduce her and criminal folly to kill her husband in order to marry her. *Bathsheba's grandfather was Ahithophel.*

One does not need to be a prophet, or the son of a prophet, to imagine how Ahithophel took the seduction of his granddaughter and the murder of her husband. He did his best to pay David back with seduction, and he succeeded. He did his best to murder David and very likely would have succeeded if Absalom had been anything like a general.

We know what David said when news of Ahithophel's treason was brought. He asked God to turn Ahithophel's counsel to foolishness. But we wonder what he said to Bathsheba, when news came to him of the suicide of Ahithophel, his old friend, his valued counselor, and Bathsheba's grandfather. What did he say? What will we say when our sins thus terribly find us out?

Devotion 21

"I HAVE COMMANDED THE RAVENS"

1 KINGS 17:1–7

The great prophet Elijah had burst like a tornado into the presence of Ahab and Jezebel. He had with him a key that could lock or unlock the sun, the rain, the wind, and the storm. Before the astonished eyes of that godless and guilty king and queen, Elijah locked up the rain. "No more rain!" he said, "No more rain but according to my word." Then he stormed back out of the royal presence and vanished from view. And he remained hidden for three and a half years while great tribulation fell on the land. "Go hide yourself," God said. Later He would say, "Go show yourself." God invariably conceals his chosen servant before He reveals that one.

During this three-and-a-half-year period, Elijah was hidden by God in a wadi and then by a widow. By the *winding brook*, Elijah developed a faith that could conquer drought. By the *wasting barrel*, in the widow's bare kitchen, Elijah developed a hope that could conquer despair. By that *widow's boy*, Elijah developed a faith that could conquer death. Once he had learned these lessons, God was able to use him as few have ever been used before or since. Israel's faith was as dry as that brook. Israel's hope was as *dismal* as that depleted barrel, and Israel's love was as *dead* as that boy. Elijah, having learned *personally* how to deal with such things, could now deal with them publicly.

But let us spend some time with the great prophet as he sits beside that drying brook in a hidden place, far from the haunts and habitations of people. And let us recall the Lord's own words to His own about the raven: "Consider the ravens," He said (Luke 12:24–28). Elijah certainly must have considered them during those days beside that brook. He looked forward to their visits twice a day.

Elijah must have considered their *color*, black and glossy. Elijah would doubtless think of the Shulamite, in Solomon's spirit-born song, and her description of her beloved: "His locks," she said, "are bushy, and black as a raven" (5:11). That reminder would take Elijah's soul by storm, for the Shulamite's words reached far beyond her own beloved. They pointed to Another, one who was yet to come, one to whom the Shulamite's beloved was but a type. Elijah's thoughts took wing. From the visiting ravens and from the shepherd-love of the Shulamite, his thoughts would soar down the centuries from the Shulamite's beloved to heaven's Beloved. So, the color of the ravens alone reminded the lonely prophet of Christ.

Then he considered their *cry*. As they dropped their tribute at his feet and wheeled away into the setting sun, Elijah would think, perhaps, of the psalmist's words, "Sing unto the LORD with thanksgiving. . . . He giveth to the beast his food, and to the young ravens which cry" (Ps. 147:7, 9). True, the ravens waited on his table in the wilds, but it was God Himself who spread the feast.

Moreover he would consider their *character*. The Levitical Law would come to his mind. Moses had specifically pronounced ravens to be unclean: "And these are they which ye shall have in abomination among the fowls . . . every raven after his kind (Lev. 11:13, 15). The raven by nature was an unclean bird.

The black, unclean birds would remind Elijah of the abomination that rode triumphant in Israel, spurred on by Jezebel and urged on by hundreds of her attendant court priests. He would take courage as he viewed the ravens coming from afar. If God could so cleanse ravens and make them ministers to His own, then there was nothing too hard for God. He had changed the very nature of these birds so that twice a day they brought him meat and bread to eat. God could change the heart of erring Israel.

Finally, the prophet would consider their *course*, as he watched them whirling and diving in the sky. He would remember the first mention of crows in the Bible. God have given them room in the ark; but, at the first opportunity, they went back to their wild, corrupt, and carnal ways. Unlike the dove, which came eagerly back to the ark from its flight abroad, the crows preferred a world where death reigned.

So, sitting by his brook, Elijah drew lessons from the ravens; and his faith grew strong. There was nothing too hard for God. The man who had thus learned to look to heaven for *food* would soon be able to look to heaven for his *fire*.

Devotion 22

A DEAD BOY

1 KINGS 17:17–24

The long and the short of it was that the boy was dead. His mother had a dead son on her hands, and she knew it. Many people have the same problem. They have children who are very much alive to all that this world has to offer, but, just the same, are spiritually dead, "dead in trespasses and sins" (Eph. 2:1). This mother had done all that a mother could do for her son, but now he was beyond all human help. She turned to the one man she knew who knew a God she did not know.

There are three people in the story: the dead boy, the distraught mother, and the distressed prophet. The problem with the boy was physical, the problem of the woman was emotional, and the problem of the prophet was spiritual. The child cried to his mother, the mother cried to the prophet, and the prophet cried to God. The tragedy in that little cottage in that pagan town gives us a glimpse of why God allows sorrow to come into our lives. For the widow, for instance, it led to confession. For Elijah it led to compassion.

For the woman, it led to *confession of sin*. We are not told what her sin was. Likely enough, it had something to do with idolatry. She was a pagan, but a pagan to whom God had spoken. The idolatry of the Canaanites involved the grossest immorality. Few could have escaped it. Perhaps the woman had once been engaged in some aspect of the immorality of her religion. Perhaps her boy was its fruit. In time, the woman had come to idolize her child. When Elijah had asked for a piece of bread, she told him that all she had was a handful of meal. "It is just enough for one small meal for me and *my son*," she said. Before it was all over, the prophet would say in the name of the living God, "Give me thy son." That is about all we can do with spiritually dead children, give them to God, totally and without reservation.

As she gazed at her dead child, a sense of her sin suddenly overwhelmed this woman: "What have I to do with thee, O thou man of God?" she cried. "Art thou come unto me to call my sin to remembrance, and to slay my son?" It suddenly dawned on her that she was a sinner, though Elijah had said nothing at all about sin. The mere presence of a truly holy person often has that effect on guilty people.

We turn now to the prophet himself. In all this, God wanted to develop within the prophet a *compassion of soul*. Elijah was the prophet of the Law and not overly famous for his grace. There was a great deal of difference, for example, between Moses and Elijah. Moses unveiled the Law, and Elijah upheld the Law. Moses interceded for *Israel*, but Elijah interceded *against* Israel. Both men were prophets; but whereas Moses was essentially a thoughtful pastor, Elijah was essentially a thundering preacher. Moses brought down food from heaven; Elijah brought down fire.

The death of the widow's boy touched the very heart of the prophet. Doubtless he had grown fond of the boy. "Give me thy son," he said in response to the widow's cry. He gathered the dead boy up in his arms (we never read of him doing that before), and carried the corpse up the stairs to his room. He placed it on his bed. Then he prayed.

His prayer consisted of just a few words. It can be said in five seconds. Truly we are not heard for our abundant words. Prayer is not measured by its length but by its depth.

Then Elijah stretched himself upon the corpse. By so doing, he stood before God as a man defiled, for the Mosaic Law pronounced all who touched a dead body to be unclean. By this act the prophet, in effect, said to God: "O God, this boy is dead, and the Law can do nothing for him. The Law cannot minister life. I therefore disqualify myself, as a man of the Law, from being able to do anything at all for this boy. If anything is to be done for this dead boy, then something above and beyond the 'Law' must take over. So I put this matter before you, not on the basis of Law, but on the basis of grace." No wonder, within minutes, he was able to say to the widow: "See, thy son liveth."

That is what we must do for our dead sons and daughters. We cannot legislate holiness or command our children to be good. Even the Law of God itself cannot impart life. But grace can, and does. Blessed be God!

Devotion 23

THE GOD THAT ANSWERETH BY FIRE

1 KINGS 18:17–46

Elijah was unique among the prophets. Obadiah was supporting no less than one hundred of them; but, one and all, they cowered in a cave in fear for their lives. Much good they were doing! Not so Elijah. He was made of sterner stuff. He was a veritable Melchizedek among the prophets, presented, as it were, without father or mother, without beginning or ending of days, a prophet of the Most High God.

Summoned into his presence, the weak and wicked king Ahab tried bluster and bravado. Elijah shut him up. "Get your priests and people to Carmel," He demanded. "We'll put things to the test." And, for the moment, more afraid of Elijah than of Jezebel, Ahab agreed. After all, Ahab thought, what could one lone man do against four hundred fifty priests and prophets of Baal? Not much!

We look first at *the cult.* The ministers of its foul and fierce rituals were an unholy crew. The hideous and polluted apostasy they championed, had it won the battle on Mount Carmel that day, would have obliterated the name and memory of Israel from the roll call of the nations. The terms of the contest were simple. The four hundred fifty prophets of Baal were to be given a bullock. And Elijah was to have one, too. Each in turn would sacrifice their animal and place it on the altar. Then the god that answered by fire would be acknowledged to be God. In growing despair, the false prophets of Baal worked themselves into a frenzy. Elijah stood by and mocked them with a fine flow of sarcasm. There lay their dead bullock on its bed of wood. There in the sky, long past its meridian, their Zidonian sun god was sinking into the sea. Baal's prophets and priests cried aloud. They slashed themselves. They worked themselves into a frenzy. All in vain. The sun continued to sink, unmoved by it all.

Now let us look at *the crowd*. All day long they had watched the antics of the Baal cult. Now it was Elijah's turn. Calmly he repaired an old mountain altar. Then deliberately he slew his bullock. He placed it on the altar. Around the altar he dug a wide trench. Then he had twelve barrels of water poured all over the altar and filled the trench as well.

The crowd gathered around as the evening shadows began to steal across the sky. Then Elijah prayed. The fire fell. It was a good thing for the people there that day that a sacrifice lay there upon the altar dressed and ready for the fire. "Our God is a consuming fire," the Bible says (Heb. 12:29). And so He is. The flame descending from on high would have landed on the people and consumed them all had there been no altar there. Instead, it fell upon the sacrifice. In type and symbol Elijah put the cross between that holy God in heaven and that sinful people on earth. The only ones who died that day were the prophets of Baal, slain by Elijah for the wickedness they had wrought.

Then came *the cloud*. The great tribulation was over! Elijah, who had just appealed to heaven for fire, now appealed to heaven for *rain*. "He prayed," the Holy Spirit says. He and his servant divided the task. The servant was to watch; Elijah was to pray. And so he did, until a cloud like a man's hand appeared in the sky, until the prophet's upraised hand left its imprint on the sky. Then down came the rain.

Obadiah's hidden prophets did not bring the rain that day. Elijah did. They could not have brought the fire either. God does not give the key of heaven and power over the forces of earth to such as they.

A SUCCESSOR FOR ELIJAH

1 KINGS 19:19

There were scores of men in Israel who would have jumped at a chance to have been Elijah's successor. Obadiah had a cave full of them. The school of the prophets had some more of them. The Spirit of God, however, passed over all of them. He already had his man in mind, one Elisha, a man with no theological training or prophetic experience at all.

There are three things to note about Elisha. First, he was a *successful farmer*. When Elijah found him, he was at work. He had twelve yoke of oxen, harnessed to a plow and was driving straight furrows across the face of a field. Elijah's heart warmed to him at once. Here was a man who had learned how to follow a plow, how to put his hand to the plow and never look back, a man fit, by the Lord's own standard, to inherit the kingdom of God. Elijah threw his mantle on him. Within the hour, Elisha had taken his plow and chopped it up for firewood. He had taken his two prize oxen and made a burnt offering of them. He had called a hasty good-bye to his family and had run as fast as he could to catch up with the master. He never looked back.

Now we look at the *submissive disciple*. He learned many things from the master while running his errands, observing his ways and sitting at his feet. He studied him. Here was a man unimpressed by the *political* establishment. Elijah had taken the measure of the Ahabs and Jezebels of this world and knew of what stuff they were made. Here was a man, moreover, totally unimpressed by the *military* establishment. Time and again whole companies of soldiers were sent to arrest him. He simply called down fire from on high to consume them. And he was equally unimpressed by the *religious* establishment. He exposed its error, deception, and weakness. Outwardly it seemed powerful, evil, and dangerous because it had the backing of the throne. Elijah exposed it as empty and devoid of spiritual power. As for the school of the prophets, Elijah long since ceased to hope for much from that source. Elijah's hopes and affections were all fixed on things above. Elisha sat at the master's feet and absorbed these things.

Finally, we see the *spiritual heir*. At length the time came for Elijah to be translated from earth to heaven (2 Kings 2). He took his journey from Gilgal to Bethel, from Bethel to Jericho, and from Jericho to the Jordan—the reverse route to that taken by Israel long years ago in its conquest of Canaan. At each stage of the journey, Elijah put his disciple to the test. Each place they came to offered an opportunity and a place of ministry. Again and again, the Master gave his disciple an opportunity to settle down, to settle for less. Each time Elisha said, "No!" He was a man trained to follow the plow, to never take his eye off the goal. And what Elisha wanted was a double portion of the master's spirit—at all costs. He had not given ten years of his life sitting at Elijah's feet in order to compromise now.

And that is what he received—a double portion of the master's spirit. Elijah performed eight miracles, Elisha performed sixteen. He was Elijah's spiritual heir.

Henceforth there was to be a man in heaven and a man on earth. The man in heaven had once lived on earth. He had trodden the path of obedience down here. He was now seated on high. The man on earth received a double portion of the Spirit of the man now in heaven. The master went up, the Spirit came down.

Henceforth the man on earth would tread the same path of obedience once trodden on earth by the man now in heaven.

The whole scene was a foreview of Christ in heaven and Christians on earth. As we live down here the life of the man up there, we too know something of the outpouring of the Spirit of God upon us. "He that believeth on me," Jesus said, "the works that I do shall he do also; and greater works than these" (John 14:12).

Devotion 25

COME DOWN

NEHEMIAH 6:3

U p went the walls! Such was the drive, the determination, and the discipline of Nehemiah that it took only fifty-two days to accomplish the task, less than two months. But it was not without opposition. One of the wiles of the foe was to try to lure Nehemiah away. We note *the proposal*: "Come," said Sanballat and Geshem to the Jewish leader. "Come, let us meet together in some one of the villages" (Neh. 6:2). The proposal would have meant a journey of at least twenty-five miles. "They thought to do me mischief," Nehemiah said. He saw right through their somewhat transparent plot.

We note also *the priority*: "I am doing a great work," said Nehemiah, "so that I cannot come down: why should the work cease, whilst I leave it, and come down to you?" (v. 3). And that was that. So far as Nehemiah was concerned, nothing mattered more than completing the repair of Jerusalem's walls.

It is important to have our priorities right. Nehemiah knew perfectly well that no meeting with the enemy could be productive because Nehemiah's priority was nonnegotiable. There are many such things that we must hold as nonnegotiable—the truth of the inerrancy of Scripture, for instance, or any of the other great cardinal doctrines of the Christian faith. There is no point in even discussing them with the enemies of the gospel since we have no room for compromise on any of these things.

Now let us note *the parallel*, for this whole story can be lifted from its Old Testament setting and put down in a New Testament one—similar but profoundly more significant. It is the same place we have in view, the city of Jerusalem, but a completely different period of time.

The scene is set on a skull-shaped hill not far from Jerusalem's wall, and the enemy is there in full force. Three crosses have been raised against the sky, and the anguish they represent can barely be imagined. On the center cross we see the Son of God. The mocking multitudes ignore the two thieves, for after all, they were just common criminals paying for their crimes. The malice of both the mob and the masters of Israel is directed toward the one who claimed to be the Son of God. The claim, they thought, was clearly incredible. But it made a good jest as well as a good test: "If thou be the Son of God," they said, "come down to us. Then we'll believe you." Nothing happened. No word passed His lips. Indeed, He had no need to speak. His answer had been on record for centuries. Nehemiah had spoken the words, and Jesus simply rested on them: "I am doing a great work," He might have said. "I cannot come down: why should the work cease, whilst I leave it, and come down to you?"

And what a great work it was! He was securing eternal salvation for a countless multitude by bearing the sins of the world in His body on the tree. He was purchasing redemption for lost Adam's fallen race. He was working out a plan agreed upon by Father, Son, and Holy Spirit before ever time began. Why, indeed, should the work cease while He came down from that cross to satisfy the idle curiosity of a disbelieving crowd? No! He stayed there, where He was, until the work was done. Then He spoke. "It is finished," He said. And so it was. We thank Him for it to this very day.

Devotion 26

"THEY THAT SEE ME"

PSALM 22:7

A bandoned by God (Ps. 22:1–6) and abhorred by mankind (vv. 7–10). Who could this be—friendless, forsaken, and betrayed by all? The answer is even more terrible than the question—God's own Son, the uncreated, self-existing, second person of the Godhead, manifest in flesh. Surely, as we stand on the threshold of this awesome Psalm 22, we should remove the shoes from our feet, for the place whereon we stand is holy ground. The one who hung there on that cross was the one who hung the stars. Those iron bolts of Rome could have become thunderbolts in His hands to annihilate His foes. Instead, we see Him exposed to *the contempt of mankind* (vv. 7–10).

They laughed Him to scorn. They made faces at Him and nodded their heads at Him. They said, "He trusted on the Lord that he would deliver him." The word used here for trusted occurs nowhere else— "Roll it on Jehovah," they said, "Roll it on Him." They jeered thus at the very time when it seemed that even God had let Him down.

Then, too, He was exposed to *the cruelty of mankind* (vv. 11–17). They surrounded Him, the psalmist said, like strong bulls of Bashan, like roaring lions, like wild dogs. The words paint a picture of His enemies circling the cross like so many wild beasts. Now one darts in with a taunt, now another pushes close with a wisecrack, then another with a curse.

Moreover, He was exposed to *the callousness of mankind* (v. 18). Now it was the turn of the soldiers. They soon tired of mocking jests and bitter taunts, and they simply turned their backs on Him. What cared they for His suffering? They had crucified people often enough before. This was just another execution. They nailed Him to the cross, dropped it into its socket with a nerve-tearing thud, then turned away to seize upon His legacy, His robe. They made short work of dividing up His garments, then they gathered around to gamble for the robe raiment angels would have worn with pride.

Had Mark Antony been there, as he had been years before at the funeral of Julius Caesar, perhaps he would have drawn special attention to that robe, as he did when he held up murdered Caesar's robe for all the world to see. Shakespeare presents Mark Antony's words as follows:

> If you have tears, prepare to shed them now.
> You all do know this mantle; I remember
> The first time ever Caesar put it on. . . .
> Look, in this place ran Cassius' dagger through:
> See what a rent the envious Casca made. . . .
> Great Caesar fell. O, what a fall was there. . . ."[1]

Did Peter, we wonder, take that robe, not in substance but in imagery, at Pentecost and spread it out, blood stained, before the people as he charged them with the murder of the Son of God? Perhaps not! But just the same he had words more eloquent, more terrible than any that Shakespeare put into the mouth of Antony. "Him . . . ye have taken," he declared, "and . . . have crucified and slain" (Acts 2:23).

All their contempt, all their cruelty, and all their callousness came home to roost at Pentecost. A Spirit-emboldened Peter preached to the suddenly awakened conscience of the Jewish people.

How wonderful that by then the contempt, the cruelty, and the callousness of people was to be answered not just in conviction and condemnation but with the infinite compassion of God. The cross was no longer just a gallows. It had become an instrument of grace.

---

1. William Shakespeare, *Julius Caesar*, act 3, scene 2.

Devotion 27

THE FLOODTIDE OF WRATH

PSALM 69:1

On April 10, 1912, the *Titanic* set out to sea. It was billed as "the unsinkable ship," some 66,000 tons of mechanics and magnificence. Five days later it sank through countless fathoms of water to the bottom of the sea. What happened? The *Titanic* struck an iceberg, which tore a three-hundred-foot gash in its side. The waters outside the ship came surging in—and the unsinkable ship was sunk.

Two thousand years ago, on a clear and starry night, in a remote Judean town, God launched a mighty vessel on the seas of time, an unsinkable ship indeed, engineered in eternity, to plans and blueprints drawn up before ever time began. The vessel itself was fashioned by the Holy Spirit in a virgin's womb. It was launched with scarcely a ripple to disturb mankind. There, in the small village of Bethlehem, the Son of God became the Son of Man.

Seas of sin surged all around Him even as He opened His eyes. A monster of a man sat on the throne that was rightfully His, a man who tried to murder Him. But the would-be killer was too late; the ship had already gone.

He grew up in an ordinary home. His brothers and sisters had sin natures just like everyone else. He, however, in stark contrast, lived a sinless life. There was no crack, no flaw to be found in Him. As man He was innocent and beyond reproof; as God He was holy and absolutely without any taint of sin.

He plowed through the seas of time until He came to Calvary, and there the iceberg struck, and the seas of sin surged into His soul. He sank swiftly. Sin (not His, but ours, for He Himself was sinless) was *destroying him*. "Save Me, O God," He said, "for the waters are come in unto my soul." He who for countless ages had known sin as an omniscient Observer now knew sin by becoming sin. "Save me!" He cried. He was answered by total silence. There was no Savior provided for Him. There was no Savior possible for Him if we were to be saved from sin.

Then, too, He felt that sin was *defiling him*. "Save me, O God . . . I sink in deep mire" (Ps. 69:1–2). It was as though all the filthiness and all the impurity of the human race had been gathered together in one vast, stinking quagmire; and He was being plunged beneath its loathsome ooze. The unbelievable horror of it had caused Him to sweat blood in Gethsemane and caused Him to cry in anguish at Golgotha.

But then, as though all that were not enough, He felt that sin was *drowning Him*: "Save me, O God . . . I am come into deep waters, where the floods overflow me." Down, down He went; and all God's billows rolled over Him. Noah, in his day, had his ark; but Jesus was left to sink, abandoned by humanity and by God. Jonah cried from "the belly of hell" and was heard. Jesus cried in vain.

"Save me!" He cried. No answer came. Instead, the tempest's voice was heard. The wind shrieked across a sunless sea, and the angry waves of wrath built themselves into marching mountains. He who once had stilled the storm with a word, who once had walked upon the angry deep, now sank beneath the waves, dragged down by the inconceivable weight of a whole world's sin.

And that seemed to be the end of it. He died and was taken down from the cross and put in a tomb. For three days and three nights the world continued to spin in space—a graveyard for His lifeless form. Then:

> Up from the grave He arose,
> With a mighty triumph o'er His foes;
> He arose a victor from the dark domain,
> And He lives forever with His saints to reign.
> He arose! He arose! Hallelujah! Christ arose![1]

---

1.   Samuel Taylor Coleridge, *The Rime of the Ancient Mariner*, 1797.

Devotion 28

LONELINESS

PSALM 102; PROVERBS 18:24; MATTHEW 27:46;
MARK 1:13; JOHN 7:53; 8:1

Samuel Taylor Coleridge is famous for having written a picturesque poem about an ancient mariner who set sail for a distant shore. An albatross followed the ship, mile after endless mile. The mariner shot it. At once the helpful wind died away, and the ship became becalmed. The sailors put two and two together. The albatross had brought the wind. Their messmate had killed the albatross. The wind had died with the bird.

In time the sailors began to die of thirst, and they died cursing the ancient mariner. At last he alone was left. There was nothing to do, nowhere to go, no one to talk to. He was alone with his remorse. As he told the wedding guest he had waylaid, he was

> Alone, alone, all, all alone,
> Alone on a wide wide sea!
> And never a saint took pity on
> My soul in agony.[1]

Loneliness is indeed a visitor to be feared. And often, once it comes, it stays. There is the loneliness of a young man, far from home and friends, wandering the shops and malls of a foreign city, surrounded by people but never a one to be his friend. There is the loneliness of a childless widow wandering the rooms of a home that has now become a house filled with dead furniture, haunting memories, and crucified hopes.

The psalmist had tasted loneliness. He describes himself as being a lost "pelican of the wilderness." A pelican belongs on a seashore, not in

---

1. Robert Lowry, "Christ Arose," 1874.

the wild wastes of the wilderness. He was like a lost owl, "like an owl of the desert," he says. An owl belongs where there are forests and fields. He was like a lost sparrow, "a sparrow alone upon the house top." A sparrow belongs in the noisy, busy fellowship of its kind (Ps. 102:6–7).

Jesus knew what it was like to be lonely. It came over Him overwhelmingly at times. In a graphic statement, unfortunately spoiled by a chapter division, we read: "Every man went unto his own house." Jesus went to the Mount of Olives (John 7:53; 8:1). Foxes had their holes, and the birds of the air had their nests; but Jesus had nowhere to lay His head.

And who among us has ever fathomed the depths of His dreadful cry on the cross: "My God, My God, why hast thou forsaken me?" (Matt. 27:46). That was at the end of his ministry. It had its echo in the dark days of His temptation at the beginning of His ministry. Mark tells us that Jesus "was there in the wilderness forty days, tempted of Satan; and was with the wild beasts" (Mark 1:13). Perhaps Satan sent them, as the Romans sent starving beasts into the arena to devour the Christians. If Satan imagined Jesus would be attacked by wild beasts, he was very much mistaken. They would be tame as lambs to Him and companions for a while in His loneliness. Then, they, too, went away; and the angels came.

By that time, the Lord was at the end of His strength, starving from a forty-day fast, exhausted from a titanic battle with the Evil One. The beasts! The angels! Where was Peter? Where was John? Where were the Twelve? He was alone.

So now, as our Great High Priest in heaven, He has a personal knowledge of what it is like to be lonely! And He does something about it. On the level of His humanity, He shows us ways out of our loneliness. He who would have friends must show himself friendly, He says (Prov. 18:24). There are millions of lonely and needy people. We can seek out some of them to befriend. And on the level of His deity, He adds: "And there is a friend that sticketh closer than a brother." Yes, indeed! What a Friend we have in Jesus, all our griefs and pains to bear! He will never leave us or forsake us. He is our faithful, unchangeable Friend.

Devotion 29

UNTO US A CHILD IS BORN

ISAIAH 9:6

"A child is born!" says Isaiah; "A son is given!" Matthew and Luke tell us of the Child that was born; John tells of the Son that was given. The child born! That points us to the Son of Man. The Son given! That points us to the Son of God. The child born was the Babe of Bethlehem; the Son given was "the Lord from heaven." The Child born reminds us that He was truly man, and the Son given tells us He was God. The Child born! That marks a beginning in time. The Son given is the Ancient of Days, from everlasting to everlasting. Jesus was both the Child born and the Son given.

The prophet gives us a fourfold description of this glorious one born of the Virgin Mary and conceived by the Holy Spirit.

He is "the wonderful counselor." That is, there is *no problem He cannot solve.* There are thousands of psychiatrists in the United States alone. People go to them to pour out their anger, frustration, bitterness, hatred, fear, envy, and guilt—and the problems in our society multiply and grow more and more horrendous all the time. Obviously psychiatrists, psychologists, social workers, and trained counselors do not have any real answers to the problems of people in general and society at large. But Jesus does! There is no problem He cannot solve. No one ever appealed to Him in vain. No one ever found Him at a loss. For in Him "are hid all the treasures of wisdom" (Col. 2:3).

Then, too, He is "the mighty God." There is *no power He cannot subdue.* He is the "Creator of the rolling spheres, ineffably sublime." He who can fling a hundred billion galaxies into space, or populate a drop of ditch water with countless microscopic germs, or pack enough power into an atom to incinerate a city can surely put down at will any power on earth or in heaven or in hell.

Moreover, there is *no period He does not span.* He is "the Father of

Eternity." We go back, ever further back in time, and always He is there. Back we go to the creation and even back beyond that. And there He is, about to launch countless stars and their satellites into vast orbits, at inconceivable velocities, to travel with mathematical precision on predictable paths! Always He is there—inescapable, gathering all time into the eternal present tense.

And, too, there is *no person He cannot save.* For the one who sits astride the centuries, who walks amid the galaxies, who has all wisdom, and who dwells amid great certainties has nail prints in His hands. He is mighty to save: "Whosoever will may come," He says. That Child born, that Son given, is our Savior and our Lord. And, blessed be God our God, He is our peace.

THE LORD AND HIS BOYHOOD

ISAIAH 53:2

There never was a boy like Jesus. Isaiah tells us two things about the boyhood of our Lord. First, He tells us *how holy He was.* He says, "He shall grow up before him as a tender plant"—that has to do with His *nature.* "And as a root out of a dry ground" has to do with His nurture. Both set Him apart from all other boys.

A tender plant! Over the years, I have preached at Park of the Palms, a retirement center in Florida. At one time, the grounds were kept beautiful by a retired professional gardener. Only once did I hear him address an audience. This is what he said:

> On a stormy night in winter, I like to pull up my chair to the fire and get out my seed catalogues and plan my garden for the coming year. All plants featured in a seed catalog are described in one of three ways. They are either *hardy, half-hardy,* or *tender.* There are some very real differences, I can assure you, between these various categories.
>
> A *hardy* plant is one native to the area. It will take ready root because it feels at home. The soil, the climate, the weather are all congenial. A *half-hardy* plant is one that is not a native to the area, but it comes from a similar environment. The conditions are much the same, so it quickly settles in as a native. But a *tender* plant—well, that's a different story. It is an exotic plant. It comes from far away. It does not find the soil or the climate congenial. It will need special attention. It will have to be protected from the weather. It will have to be fed special nutrients. It is a tender plant.
>
> Our Lord Jesus was in this sin-cursed world as a tender plant. He came from far away. His nature was not like our nature. This world's sin-ridden social, secular, and spiritual climate was foreign to Him. He was holy and harmless and undefiled and separate from sinners.

He was a transplant from glory. He came out of eternity into time. As man, He was absolutely innocent; as God, He was absolutely holy. He was holy even as a boy. He was good, as God is good. He had no sin nature. "Satan cometh," He said, toward the end of His life. "Satan cometh and hath nothing in me." He was a tender plant from another land, a land beyond the sky. He was a transplant from Glory. This sin-cursed world of ours was not His real home.

The prophet goes on to describe His *nurture*. By the time Jesus came to earth, the major pagan world religions had long since been founded and given a chance to show what mere religion can do. The Lord found nothing in them. The great philosophers of Greece had come and gone and been given their chance to deal with the human condition. The Lord found nothing to nurture Him in them. Judaism had abandoned the Torah for the budding Talmud—the Mishnah and the Midrash had already taken deep root. There was nothing to nurture Him there—just the opinions and traditions of men. So he drove His roots deep into the Word of God. He was a root, indeed, out of a dry ground. He became the blessed man of Psalm I, the tree planted by the rivers of water, by the Spirit of God Himself. Isaiah tells us, moreover, *how human He was*. He was God incarnate, burning with holiness but all His essential, innate glory was so veiled by His humanity that the prophet could add: "He hath no form nor comeliness; and when we shall see him, there is no beauty that we should desire him." All people saw was "the carpenter's son." They saw a man in a homespun robe, speaking the local dialect, and they dismissed Him as a Galilean peasant. They saw no beauty in Him at all. Indeed, the people of His native village tried to kill Him for telling them the truth. But God's eye was on Him. The angels were watching over Him. He was God's "tender plant," a transplant from another world, cultivated and protected by God while living in a hostile world.

Devotion 31

HE AND ME

ISAIAH 53:4–6

He and me! It is not very good grammar, perhaps, but it is very good gospel. Let us read what the prophet says, putting the emphasis on ourselves.

"Surely he hath borne *our* griefs, and carried *our* sorrows. . . . He was wounded for *our* transgressions, he was bruised for *our* iniquities: the chastisement of *our* peace was upon him; and with his stripes *we* are healed. . . . *We* have turned every one to his own way; and the LORD hath laid on him the iniquity of *us* all." Amazing! All for us.

But the statement becomes all the more amazing when we turn it around and put all the emphasis on Him.

"Surely *he* hath borne our griefs, and carried our sorrows. . . . *He* was wounded for our transgressions, *he* was bruised for our iniquities: the chastisement of our peace was upon *him*; and with *his* stripes we are healed. . . . We have turned every one to his own way; and the LORD hath laid on *him* the iniquity of us all." As the hymn says,

> And when I think that God, His *Son* not sparing,
> Sent *Him* to die, I scarce can take it in,
> That on the cross, my burden gladly bearing,
> *He* bled and died to take away my sin.[1]

"He was wounded for our *transgressions*," the prophet declares. There are five kinds of wounds we can suffer. There is a *contused* wound, one that results from a blow delivered by a blunt instrument. The Lord suffered that kind of a wound when they blindfolded Him, and some brute of a man drew back his fist and punched Him with all his force in the face.

---

1. Carl Boberg, "How Great Thou Art," 1885.

There is a *laceration*, the kind of wound produced by a tearing instrument. The Lord suffered terrible lacerations when He was scourged. A Roman scourge was a fearful thing. The victim was bound to a post and beaten with a whip of numerous cords in which were embedded bits of iron or bone. The flesh was torn off the back and the organs exposed. It was not uncommon for a man to die under a scourging.

Then, too, there is a *penetrating* wound, a wound produced by a sharp-pointed instrument. The Lord suffered this kind of wound when He was crowned with thorns. The Jerusalem thorn has spikes four inches long. The mocking crown was pressed down upon His head producing a ring of wounds around His brow, deepened by subsequent blows to His head.

There is also a *perforating* wound, the kind of wound caused when the instrument pierces right through. The Lord suffered this wound when they pierced His hands and His feet.

Finally, there is an *incision* resulting from a cut produced by a sharp-edged instrument such as a knife or a sword. The last indignity done to the Lord's body was done with a Roman spear. That great gash in His side showed Him to be dead. So we sing:

> Wounded for me, wounded for me,
> There on the cross He was wounded for me;
> Gone my transgressions, and now I am free,
> All because Jesus was wounded for me.[2]

When we sing that, we picture Him receiving all the wounds we can experience. Moreover, He carries the scars of those wounds to this very day, up there in glory, to the wonder of the redeemed and all the hosts of heaven.

---

2. W. G. Ovens, "Wounded for Me."

Devotion 32

BEHOLD, MY SORROW

LAMENTATIONS 1:12

Is it nothing to you, all ye that pass by? Behold, and see if there be any sorrow like unto my sorrow, which is done unto me, wherewith the LORD hath afflicted me in the day of his fierce anger."

We think first of the *primary* application of these words. They were spoken by Jeremiah, the weeping prophet of the Old Testament. All about him was a desolate, depopulated, and devastated city. The Babylonians had torn it to pieces, destroyed its glorious temple, deported its people, and defied its God. So much for all Jeremiah's preaching! He had been reviled and afflicted by his own people, and now he roamed the corpse-strewn ruins of Jerusalem, abandoned to his grief. So great were his sorrows that a special book of the Bible was set apart to record them, the book of Lamentations. Truly *Jeremiah* was a man of sorrows.

We think, next, of the *peripheral* application of these words. Indeed, there are others whose stories are treasured up within the bounds of God's book, people who learned through sufferings.

There was *Joseph*, for instance. Doubtless, by the time of his mother's death, Joseph had learned to be afraid of his older brothers. They hated him and could not speak peaceably to him. As cautious as he had become, however, it is doubtful that he was prepared for their final, united onslaught on him. He never thought he would be flung into a pit, his princely mantle torn from his shoulders, and his fate fiercely debated by his brothers; and with murder on his brothers' minds, the prospect of being hauled from the pit and sold into slavery in a foreign land never occurred to him. And then, once in that faraway land, he was falsely accused and flung into prison and left there to rot! Such were the sufferings of Joseph.

Then there was *Jonah*. True, he brought his suffering on himself; but it was nonetheless real and terrible. We can scarcely imagine the horror of his situation, to be swallowed alive and lost in the vast interior of a great fish, to be in the dark, awash with the debris of a great sea creature's meals, to be scorched by its gastric juices, to be overwhelmed by the heat, and to be suffocated by the smell. No wonder he called it "the belly of hell" (Jonah 2:2). And the torment went on for three days and three nights. Certainly Jonah came very near to death. Such were the sufferings of Jonah.

And what about Job? Sorrow after sorrow surged in upon his soul, until—wealth gone, health gone, family gone, friends gone—he felt that God Himself had become his enemy. And all this for no apparent reason and, it seemed, with no foreseeable end. His friends hotly debated the cause of Job's suffering and concluded that they could only be explained in terms of some horrendous secret sin in Job's life—a conclusion he vehemently denied. Nobody divined the true cause of Job's torment, or the triumphant conclusion that would be his. Such were the sufferings of Job.

This brings us to the *prophetic* application of these words: "Is it nothing to you, all ye that pass by? Behold, and see if there be any sorrow like unto my sorrow, which is done unto me, wherewith the LORD hath afflicted me in the day of his fierce anger." The sufferings of Jeremiah, the sufferings of Joseph, the sufferings of Jonah, and the sufferings of Job all pale before the sufferings of *Jesus*. Like Jeremiah, Jesus wept over Jerusalem. Like Joseph, He came unto His own, and His own received Him not. Like Jonah, all God's waves and billows passed over Him, and He cried in utter desperation and desolation in total darkness. And, like Job, His sufferings were all undeserved. There was no sorrow like His.

Who can even begin to imagine the sufferings of Jesus when He, who knew no sin, was made sin for us? Only God can know the full measure of that. Well might we borrow the language of the old hymn:

> Oh, make me understand it,
> Help me to take it in;
> What it meant for Thee, the Holy One
> To take away my sin.[1]

I. Katharine A. M. Kelly, "O Make Me Understand It."

Devotion 33

THE RIVER

EZEKIEL 47:1–12

The scene here is millennial. Its scope is monumental. Ezekiel's closing end-time visions are focused on the awesome temple yet to grace the earth when Jesus will reign "from the river unto the ends of the earth" (Ps. 72:8). It is the river that thrills the prophet here. It flows out from the temple, and it brings life and loveliness everywhere it goes. Obviously, however, there must be more to it than that. And so there is.

In the Bible, God the Father is likened to a *fountain* of living water (Jer. 2:13). God the Son is likened to a *well* of living water (John 4:14), and God the Holy Spirit is likened to a *river* of living water (John 7:37–39).

The eighth day of the Feast of Tabernacles was always a Sunday. It was kept as a special Sabbath, and it was the great, climactic conclusion of all the festivities of the year. On each of the first seven days, the priests brought vessels of water from the pool of Siloam and poured them out in a river over the steps of the temple. Jesus seized upon this activity to introduce His people to the Holy Spirit, who was soon to replace Him on earth as resident member of the Godhead.

Coming back now to the end-time river Ezekiel saw coming out of the future millennial temple, there are four things we can learn about the river of the Spirit. Note, first, *the general direction of the river.* The prophet stepped into this life-giving stream until the water was to his ankles. His walk was now controlled by the river. Where it went, he went. He followed its leading, treading a path of obedience. It was the path that Jesus trod from the virgin womb of Mary in Bethlehem to the virgin tomb of Joseph in Jerusalem. It is that path of obedience we must tread if we would know more of the Spirit of God.

We note, also, *the growing dominance of the river.* The prophet walked out a thousand cubits deeper into the river. The water was now to his knees. The knees remind us of *submission*—"Every knee should bow," Paul says (Phil. 2:10–11)—and they remind us of *supplication*, for we bend our knees when we pray. Water to the knees brings us into deeper experience of the Holy Spirit. How little we know about praying in the Holy Spirit. "We know not what we should pray for as we ought," Paul says (Rom. 8:26–27). The Holy Spirit must help our infirmities in this regard.

We note, next, *the great dynamic of the river*. Another thousand cubits into the river, and the water reaches to the loins. The full force of the river can now be felt. In Scripture the loins refers to the lower part of the back, the pivot of the whole body. The loins also refers to the seat of generative power, the seat of life. To have one's "loins girt" in the Bible means to be ready for vigorous effort. Water to the loins takes us to an even deeper knowledge of the Holy Spirit as the one who provides power for service and for bringing people to the new birth.

Finally, we note *the glorious design of the river*. Another thousand cubits into the river and the prophet is in deep water—"waters to swim in." When we swim we surrender ourselves wholly to the water. Our feet no longer cleave to the earth. Our whole body is at the disposal of the flowing stream. Moreover, when a person is swimming, all that can be seen is the person's head. *That* is the glorious design of the Holy Spirit—that we should be so submerged in His will that all that can be seen is Jesus, our Head. We are thus borne along by the Spirit, buoyed up by the Spirit, and blessed by the Spirit of God. The result will be cleansing and fruitfulness everywhere.

Devotion 34

HOSEA

HOSEA 1:1–11

A century and a half had come and gone since Jeroboam I had torn ten of the tribes away from the throne of David to form the northern kingdom of Israel. Some fourteen kings had come and gone. Some had been weak, some had been warlike, but all had been wicked. Jeroboam had set the trend. He introduced the cult of the golden calf. It was a bad beginning. Later on, Ahab had introduced Jezebel and promoted the false worship of Baal. Now Jeroboam II was on the throne and, though outwardly strong, he had been weighed in the balance and found wanting, so God sent along a prophet, Hosea by name. His task was to show the king, the court, and the country just what God thought of them all.

The prophet had a *tragedy in his home life*. It was a full-length portrait of the *tragedy in his homeland*. A look at what Hosea's home life was like tells us all we need to know as to what his homeland was like. Hosea had no illusions regarding the state of his homeland. It was apostate.

As a young preacher, Hosea felt the need for a wife, someone to support him and to share with him in what he was sure would be a difficult ministry. The Spirit of God confirmed his leading and, shortly afterward, Hosea met Gomer. Probably the kind of wife Hosea envisioned for himself was someone like Sarah or Miriam or Jochabed or Deborah, some strong believer in God.

But his choice was Gomer. It seemed a good enough choice, for her name meant "completion." No doubt he thought she would complete him, bringing strength where he felt weakness, goodness where he was inclined to stray. So Gomer won his heart, and God confirmed to him that she was the one he should marry. What a shock he received! "A wife of whoredoms" is the Holy Spirit's later assessment of her. She was a woman given to a promiscuous lifestyle.

Whether Hosea knew it or not, we cannot be sure. If he did, doubtless he deluded himself into thinking he would change her. After all, Rahab had been a harlot, but she became a true mother in Israel and a giant of the faith. Gomer, however, broke Hosea's heart.

That was the supreme truth he was to show to Israel. He became a man of sorrows, acquainted with grief. He was married to a wife of whoredoms. Painfully he learned that sin not only breaks God's laws; it breaks God's heart. So Hosea married Gomer. The tragedy in his home life had begun.

A boy was born, and the prophet called him Jezreel. Jezreel was the name of a place of fearful associations. Naboth's vineyard had been there. The battle of Armageddon will be fought there.

But by now, Gomer was tired of restraint, and Hosea had to put up with her moods. In time, a second child was born. Hosea had grave doubts as to this girl's parentage, so he called her "Lo-ruhamah." The name means "not loved" and suggests she never knew a father's love. Then Gomer became a woman of the streets, and Hosea disowned her third child altogether. "Lo-Ammi" ("not my people") he called this boy, indicating he was no child of the prophet. The names of these children were prophetic messages addressed to apostate Israel. They warned of vengeance, of being strangers to God, and of being disowned by Him.

Gomer sank deeper and deeper into the mire until she gave herself up totally to vice. Then she became a drunkard and sold herself into prostitution. Hosea loved her still. In the end, he bought her from her owner for a few pennies—all she was worth—and took her to his home. He cleaned her up and gave her a bed. "I've bought you," he told her. "I still love you. But I don't want a slave. It's a wife that I want. I know how to wait."

Thus God loved Israel, and thus He loves the world. "[Love] suffereth long, and is kind," He says (1 Cor. 13:4). His love never lets us go. It pursues us even into the far country. "His love knows no limit to its endurance, no end to its trust," as one translator puts it. It never fails.

Devotion 35

JOEL

Joel looms up out of nowhere, raises his voice, and then vanishes back into the shadows. He seems to have been the very first of the writing prophets. He wrote six dozen verses, that's all. But for all that, this so-called *minor* prophet was the herald of a *major* departure in the prophetic world. Joel wrote things down.

Shakespeare makes the envious Cassius say about Julius Caesar: "Why, man, he doth bestride the narrow world like a Colossus."[1] The same could have been said of Joel.

Two days occupied Joel—just two days. The first was *the day of the locust*. There had been rumors in Israel of a brewing plague in the southeastern deserts of the Middle East. Then one day the sky turned black and the locusts arrived. They descended by the millions on farm and field and forest. They covered the ground to a depth of one and a half feet. They ate every stalk and every stem, every leaf and every twig. "Incarnate hunger" best describes what they were. When at last they moved on, they left utter devastation in their wake. It was a divine visitation and a herald of more to come.

Then there was *the day of the Lord*. Half a dozen prophets talk about this day, but it was Joel who mentioned it first. Four concepts whirled in Joel's mind as he thought of this great judgment to come.

First, there were *fading voices*. It was only a matter of decades since the days of Elijah and Elisha. These two men, armed with might and miracle, had been a nine-day wonder in Israel. People remembered their miracles; but few remembered their message. Joel saw the need to write things down, to give people something more important than miracles, to give them a book.

---

1.   William Shakespeare, *Julius Caesar*, act I, scene 2.

The comfortable little Palestinian world was changing, and the age of the superpowers had arrived. The hostile neighboring countries of Moab and Edom and the like were nothing compared with Assyria, Babylon, Greece, and Rome. Joel saw it coming on the wings of the wind: the destruction, the desolation, and the deportation, all the inevitable fruit of apostasy. God's people would need something to hold on to. So, where Elijah produced miracles, Joel produced a manuscript.

Then there were *former values*. God had planned for Israel to be located on the crossroads of continents so that they might be a testimony to all mankind, the world's schoolmaster to bring people from many nations to Christ. A century of liberal theology, however, had rendered Israel apostate and impotent. The old landmarks had been removed, the old faith had been replaced, and the old values had been erased. It called for judgment.

So now the nation faced *fearful vengeance*. Had Israel remained true to its call, these Gentile superpowers would have come; but they would have come, not as warriors, but as worshipers. Before it was too late, Israel must repent. It was still not too late in Joel's day, but it was "repent—or else!"

But Joel still had some good news. There were to be *future visitations*. His most important prophecy had to do with an outpouring of the Holy Spirit. It took eight hundred years for Joel's prophecy of Pentecost to be fulfilled. But the outpouring did come, and we are living in the reality of it to this day. "Thank you, Joel. There was nothing *minor* about you!"

Devotion 36

AMOS

AMOS 3:3

In the days of Amos, both Israel and Judah appeared to be prosperous. Jeroboam II ruled Israel; and King Uzziah, one of Judah's handful of godly kings, reigned in Jerusalem. But it was all deceptive. Corruption and decay had advanced to the point in Israel where there was no remedy. Judgment was inevitable. Temporary revivals in Judah would postpone that country's fall, but the rot had already gone too deep in Israel.

When *revival* is no longer an option, God sends *ruin*. Already, over the distant northern skyline, the Assyrian army was preparing to march. Its arrival would bring vengeance, and Amos knew it to be so. For centuries Israel and Judah had been made up of fighting farmers. Theirs had been a rural economy and lifestyle. Life had been generally simple and wholesome. But now society had become urbanized, sophisticated, and worldly-wise. It was a situation that heralded judgment to come. Amos himself was a farmer. He was also very poor. He was what we would call a cowboy or a herdsman. His hometown was perched on the edge of a fearful desert. What he saw of urban society shocked and outraged him. We can imagine the effect he had on high society in sophisticated Samaria when he came clomping into the halls of polite people in his cowboy boots and when he addressed the cultured court women as "ye kine of Bashan" (4:1)—that is, "you barnyard cows!"

Nevertheless, we suspect that he was received, at first, with some enthusiasm in Israel, for he began by denouncing the surrounding cities and nations of Damascus, Gaza, Tyre, Edom, Ammon, Moab, and even Judah. But when he turned on Israel, it was a different story. The Israelites were furious.

By the time his scathing tongue lashed out at them, the Israelites recognized his formula—"For three transgressions . . . and for four." It expressed a Hebrew idiom. It means that the cup of God's wrath was not only full; it was more than full.

Amos was fond of using illustrations, usually drawn from desolate desert scenes familiar to him since boyhood days. For instance, he remembered once seeing a shepherd saving from the maw of a glutted lion all that was left of a sheep—a pair of shinbones and the tattered fragment of an ear (3:12). That was all. And *that* was what Israel could look forward to, when the Assyrians were finished with them.

He pictures, also, a city after the army of Assyria had ravished it. He describes a house of ten family members with only one survivor. He sees that wretched man, ravished by the plague, cowering in some dark corner. A relative comes to burn the bodies of the dead; but the relative hovers outside, afraid to go in lest he, too, should catch the plague. He calls. The sole survivor is terrified. He is afraid that the echoing voice will precipitate some new horror. "Hush!" he says. "Be quiet" (6:9–10).

Like Joel and others, Amos saw *the day of the Lord* and pictures the terror of end-time events. He sees a man fleeing from a lion, only to run into the arms of a bear. He pictures a fleeing man leaning, exhausted, against a wall, only to be bitten by a serpent. He sees a man praying; but, alas, he does not know God, and the Bible is, to him, an unknown book. How can he pray (5:19–23)?

All this was the end result of the calf cult that had slowly poisoned the whole northern kingdom. It had been founded on a wholesale application of Bible-twisting, liberal theology. No wonder that the sight of the golden calf in Bethel gave wings to the prophet's words. So, where Hosea preached love, Amos preached law. While Hosea was full of feeling, Amos was full of facts. Where Hosea went into his house for his illustrations, Amos scoured the nations and the wilds.

If God were to send a modern cowboy to stalk the halls of Congress and the White House with a message for America, what would that man say? He would probably simply preach what Amos preached—wrath! Wrath is already on the way.

Devotion 37

MICAH

MICAH 7:18

"Who is like Jehovah?" That is what *Micah* means. Evidently his parents wanted to make sure that Micah never forgot that truth. He was reminded of it every time he heard or wrote his name—"*Who is like Jehovah?*" The answer obviously was no one, especially not the false gods of the heathen!

He came from Moresheth, a town on the Philistine border and, therefore, constantly threatened by those ancient foes of Israel. And besides the words that he spoke, that is all we know about this man, just his name and his address, and the fact that he was a prophet.

We can sense his reaction when God called him: "Me? Why do you want me? After all, you've got Isaiah, and he's a very big prophet indeed. Moreover, he is cousin to the king, he has friends in high places, he is eloquent in the Scriptures, and he has a tremendous grasp of current events. Why do you want me?" The answer, of course, was that the Old Testament Law required a twofold witness before truth could be established.

Already the shadow of Assyria lay over the land of the Hebrew people. Weak King Ahaz of Judah, alarmed by the alliance of Syria and Israel against him, and disdainful of Isaiah's warnings, had appealed to Assyria for help. It was a foolish thing to do, like inviting the cat into the cage to keep peace between the canaries.

But if the Assyrians were coming, so was God. His feet would soon be "trampling out the vintage where the grapes of wrath were stored."[1] The worship of Baal, of foul Ashtaroth, and of fierce Moloch had taken over the land. God was coming in wrath. The earth had already begun to shake beneath His feet. Volcanoes erupted. The stones cried out. And dark was His path on the wings of the storm.

---

1. Julia W. Howe, "Battle Hymn of the Republic," 1861.

The swirling vortex of the approaching storm was directed at Samaria—beautiful Samaria, drowning in the vileness, the violence, and the vanity of its false and futile faiths. Its massive temple of Baal had been paid for by the hire of her harlot priestesses.

Worse still, all this religious infamy had now been imported into Judah. And neither godly King Hezekiah nor the great and gifted prophet Isaiah could stem the rising tide of wickedness in the land.

Even while Micah was preaching, weak King Ahaz, father of Hezekiah, was busy importing a pagan altar from Damascus. Solomon's great brazen altar was to be pushed out of the way and this heathen altar installed in its place.

No wonder the Assyrians were coming. The prophet made puns of the place names, places in the path of the coming conqueror, puns such as: "rolling in the dust at Dust-Town"; "falsehoods paid for at False-Town"; and so on (1:10, 14). There was, however, another town that told a better tale and Micah is the one who put that town forever on the map. The town was Bethlehem! There, in that little backwoods Judean town, the Christ of God would one day enter into human life. Micah said so.

Then Micah remembered an unrecorded and almost forgotten fragment of an old Bible tale. It was the story of Balaam, the Mesopotamian psychic, and his wily employer, King Balak of Moab. Moses had told the tale of Balaam and his sins, his sermons, and his final suggestion. But Micah remembered another sermon this pagan prophet preached. "What would God take as fair payment for my sins?" the King of Moab asked. Then, like a desperate man haggling for something he desires, the king kept on raising his offer. Finally, he reached his limit. He would give his firstborn son on the altar of sacrifice; the fruit of his body for the sin of his soul. "If you wish to buy your salvation, my lord king," the prophet had replied, "then do justly, love mercy, and walk humbly before God." This was God's message to His people. But it was too late for Israel. Judgment was on the way.

Micah makes one more pun before he puts down his pen, a pun, indeed, on his very own name: "Who is a God like unto thee, that . . . delighteth in mercy." This was the rainbow shining forth on the wings of the storm, the promise of grace in the midst of wrath to come.

Devotion 38

NAHUM

NAHUM 1:1-3

In the year 664 B.C. the great Egyptian city of Thebes fell to the Assyrians. It was a great triumph for Assyrian arms. Indeed, it seemed as though there would be no end to Assyria's nightmare victories. But an unknown Hebrew prophet, Nahum by name, felt the fire of divine inspiration burn in his soul. "Yet fifty years and Assyria would be overthrown!" That was his cry.

He saw it all. He saw the gradual formation of a coalition of Gentile nations that had long plotted vengeance on Assyria. He saw the mobilization of allied armies, united now against the common foe. He saw the collapse of Assyria's outposts and the withdrawal of the Assyrians behind the walls of Nineveh. He saw the strategies of the allied forces. And *then* he saw the sudden, catastrophic, chaotic crash of the crudest empire the world had ever known. Nahum saw it all. Over a hundred years earlier, Jonah had preached just such an overthrow to the great Assyrian city of Nineveh, but the judgment had been stayed by repentance. How Jonah would have envied Nahum, for now the time for mercy was past. Assyria had crossed that fateful boundary line God draws around such wicked empires, and its doom was sealed.

The roll call of Assyria's kings was the roll call of cruelty and carnage. There was Shalmaneser III, who called himself, "The Mighty King"; and Tiglath-Pilesar III, who turned Assyria into a superpower. There was Shalmaneser V, who invaded Israel and laid siege to Samaria; and Sargon II, who put an end to Israel and deported ten of the tribes. There was Sennacherib, the fiendishly cruel king who invaded Judah but whose army God smote before the gates of Jerusalem. There was Esarhaddon, who carried victorious Assyrian armies into Egypt and humbled wicked King Manasseh in the dust. There was Ashurbanipal, who captured Thebes and stirred Nahum's soul so that, set on fire by

God, he proclaimed the utter ruin of Assyria fifty years before the event, and at a time when the evil empire seemed all victorious. It was a long and dark, blood-soaked, terrifying chapter of history that the Assyrians left behind.

There was no end to the horrors. Captured nobles were flayed alive. Captives were burned. Prisoners of war were impaled on stakes. And it had gone on and on for over two centuries. No wonder Nahum called Nineveh "the bloody city" (3:1). No wonder, too, that a vast and heartfelt sigh of relief went up from all the surrounding countries when the news finally came—Nineveh was no more! Never again would Assyria's dreaded army march out of Nineveh's gates to torment the cities of the ancient world.

"The LORD is slow to anger," said Nahum. Nineveh itself was proof of that. "The Lord is slow to anger, and great in power, and will not at all acquit the wicked" (1:3). He added some further words. Nineveh was to be "empty, and void, and waste" (2:10).

The sun of Nineveh sank swiftly when the time came. Within fifty years of its fall, all the commerce of the world, which had beaten a path to its door, fell back into its old, familiar routes. Nineveh was lost to history, and its very location became but a vague memory.

Nahum teaches us that "the mills of God grind slowly, yet they grind exceeding small."[1] As Nebuchadnezzar learned, "The heavens *do* rule" (Dan. 4:26).

---

1. Henry Wadsworth Longfellow, "Retribution," 1870.

Devotion 39

HABAKKUK

HABAKKUK 3:18–19

Habakkuk looms up in the darkness that covered the land of Judah when wicked King Manasseh sat upon the throne. He looks about him. He lodges a bitter complaint at the supreme court of heaven. He listens in astonishment to the answer he gets. He looks about him some more. He laughs suddenly, then vanishes back into the shadows, leaving us with one great truth: the just shall live by faith.

In fact, Habakkuk seems to have been more concerned about solving a problem than in delivering a prophecy. We note *the silence of God that caused his problem*. It is a problem as old as mankind. Why does God remain silent when wickedness seems to be triumphant everywhere?

Manasseh, the son of godly King Hezekiah, was the longest reigning and wickedest of all the Judean kings. The nation never recovered from his apostasies. The calf cult was given full and free reign. The worship of Baal was supported by the throne. The Assyrian and Chaldean worship of the sun, the moon, and the stars was in vogue, along with a full-fledged belief in astrology. And there, in the temple court itself, was the Asherah, towering up like a beacon, a shameless sex object, glorifying lust. And, worst of all, the terrible worship of Moloch had the king's complete support. Such was Manasseh's Jerusalem.

And God was silent. No wonder Habakkuk was perplexed, especially as all this moral and spiritual collapse had come swiftly on the heels of Hezekiah's great reforms. This brings us to *the statement of God that compounded his problem*.

"Don't worry!" God said to his puzzled prophet. "I have already prepared my answer to your problem. I am going to hand Judah over to the Babylonians!" Habakkuk was more horrified than ever. The cure was worse than the complaint. Judah was sinful, for sure, but the Babylonians were a thousand times worse. The solution made no sense at all. This, in turn, brings us to *the sovereignty of God that canceled the problem*.

God told his servant that He knew all about the Babylonians. He knew about their greed, their goals, their guilt, their guile, and their gods. "Don't worry about the Babylonians," He declared. "Their doom is only a matter of time."

The prophet was taught that when contemplating the equation of God's dealings with the human race, he must always take two factors into consideration. First there was the *time* factor. God's calendar is far bigger than ours. He is always on time.

Then, too, he must take into account, the *trust* factor. "Trust Me," God said. "The just shall live by his *faith*" (2:4). So much for the Babylonian issues.

But now for the broader issue. God enlarged the vision of his servant and gave him a glimpse of end-time events, events that far eclipsed the events of his own day. And suddenly, Habakkuk broke into song.

"The just shall live by faith." As the truth of it got hold of the prophet, it put a spring into his step and a song into his soul. It will do the same for us.

Devotion 40

ZEPHANIAH

ZEPHANIAH 1:14–16

Zephaniah's name means "hidden by Jehovah." We must never forget that we live on a conquered planet, that its prince and god is fallen Lucifer, and that he nurses, in the deep, dark dungeons of his being, an implacable hatred for God and for His people. It is not unusual for God's people to have to be hidden. Moses was hidden by his mother. Elijah was hidden by God. Jesus Himself was hidden. Of the thirty-three and a half years Jesus lived on earth, thirty of them were hidden years.

Zephaniah was hidden. He had a secret, and it was, of necessity, a closely guarded secret. He was a great-grandson of godly King Hezekiah. During the long reign of wicked King Manasseh, it would have been as good as a death warrant to let a secret like that be known. Now that good King Josiah was on the throne, seeking to undo the damage Manasseh and Amon had done, it had suddenly become an asset to be related to the throne. So, after hiding this family secret for three generations, now in the fourth generation it could be made known. And that is how Zephaniah begins. He proclaims his royal lineage.

The *hiding* gives place to the *haunting*. There was a ghost, a grim and ghastly one at that, that haunted the prophet Zephaniah. He had another secret, and it was one that could not be hidden. What haunted Zephaniah was his particular vision of "the day of the Lord." That day, first injected into the prophetic picture by Joel, is mentioned twenty times in the Old Testament and four times in the New. It was Zephaniah who clearly saw that the day of the Lord was to be equated with the end times. He calls it "the day of the LORD's anger" (2:2), a day when *war*, *weather*, and *woe* combine to shake this planet to its core.

And suddenly there was *horror*. For coming back to the present from one of his excursions into the far future, Zephaniah saw something else that struck terror in his soul. All about him was evidence of the damage done to the nation by Manasseh, damage good King Josiah could never hope to repair. Then Zephaniah saw it. He cried out. "The just LORD is in the midst," he declared (3:5). The living God had come in person to collect fuel for the fire of His wrath, and what He saw made Him determined. He would cut good King Josiah short in his prime and remove Judah's last hope of salvation. Then He wrote "bankrupt" over Judah's account and sealed its doom.

But even so, there was *hope*. The prophet realized, at last, that there was another side to things. The day of the Lord will not just terminate at Megiddo in chaos and carnage. It will carry on to the golden age of the millennial kingdom.

So, at last, there will be *happiness*. "Sing!" he cried. "Shout! Be glad! Rejoice!" (3:14).

> Dark, dark hath been the midnight,
> But dayspring is at hand,
> And glory, glory dwelleth
> In Emmanuel's land.[1]

---

1.   Anne Ross Cousin, "The Sands of Time Are Sinking," 1857.

Devotion 41

JESUS IN THE MIDST

MATTHEW 18:20

In the midst! That is where Jesus belongs, at the center of things. Here are some occasions when we see Him in the midst.

We see Him, first, in the midst of *the curious rabbis of Jerusalem*. They did not know who He was. All they saw was a thoughtful boy, and they were used to thoughtful boys. They had been thoughtful boys once themselves.

These men were the descendants and the spiritual heirs of the handful of Jews who had come back from Babylon fired by thoughts of a building and a book. But it was the book that dominated their lives once the building, a temple for their God, was built. They began to tinker with the book until, in time, their commentaries and traditions became the Talmud. Even in its earliest forms it all but replaced God's Word in their thoughts. Now, in their midst, in fashion as a boy, stood one who was none other than the Author of the Book, the Divine Lawgiver of Sinai. He sat there among them, "both hearing them, and asking them questions" (Luke 2:46); and they knew Him not. How sad to read the Bible and not to know the very One it is all about.

We see Him, too, in the midst of *the crucified robbers at Calvary*. Hardly anyone seemed to know just who He was. Caiaphas looked at Him and saw a *menacing problem*. "We'll just have to get rid of Him," he said, "or He'll start a war with Rome and we'll lose our authority and power."

Herod looked at Him and saw a *miserable preacher*. He had heard of Him from afar. He had his own views as to who He was. He hoped to see Him perform a miracle, a clever piece of magic. He questioned Him eagerly. All he received back was a stony silence. Jesus had nothing to say to this godless man, the man who had murdered His friend. Herod was enraged and began to cover Him with abuse. The man who had murdered John now mocked Jesus.

Pilate looked at Him and saw a *misguided pretender*, one who claimed to be the King of the Jews. Pilate knew what Caesar expected him to do with rival kings. He must crucify them—so, off to Calvary with Him, in the fitting company of a couple of thieves! And, wonder of wonders, one of those thieves figured it out. This Man in the midst was the Messiah Himself; at once he owned Him to be both Savior and Lord.

Finally, we see Jesus in the midst of the *crowned royalties of heaven*. John, caught up into heaven, had trouble finding Him at first. He had been so taken up with the sights and sounds of glory that he failed to see the Lord. But, there He was, in the midst—in the midst of the throne and of the chanting cherubim and of the adoring elders.

But there is one more thought. Today He is in the midst of the *converted remnant of earth*—"Where two or three are gathered together in my name," He says, "there am I in the midst of them" (Matt. 18:20). But all too often we fail to see Him. The hymn writer says,

> If now, with eyes defiled and dim,
> We see the signs, but see not Him,
> Oh may His love the scales displace,
> And bid us see Him face to face![1]

I.   Charles H. Spurgeon, "Amidst Us Our Beloved Stands," 1866.

Devotion 42

THE DAYS OF NOAH

MATTHEW 24:37–39

Jesus said that the last days prior to His coming again will be just like the days of Noah. Those days, described in Genesis 4–6, reveal seven characteristics of the days of Noah that are also characteristics of our own day and age. First, they were days of *spiritual decline*. The faith that had been delivered to Adam—that faith for which the martyr Abel was prepared to shed his blood, and which had been distorted by Cain into a false religion—had largely disappeared in Noah's day. Those who knew the true and living God were becoming an ever-increasing minority in this world (Gen. 7:1).

The days of Noah were not only days of spiritual decline, but they were also days of *social dilemma*. This was marked by a population explosion ("men began to multiply," Gen. 6:1) and by a corresponding increase in crime. God put people in a garden. Cain put them in a city (4:17). And the great cities of the world, bursting with people, became jungles of crime. "The earth," God says, "was filled with violence" (6:11).

Then, too, the days of Noah were days of *shameless depravity*. There was polygamy, for instance. God's laws for marriage were set aside (4:19). And there was pornography, for "every imagination . . . was only evil continually" (6:5).

Next, the days of Noah were days of *scientific development*. Tremendous strides were being taken in science, technology, and engineering. The ark, believed to be as big as some of our modern oceangoing liners, was built by Noah and his helpers. The engineers of that day had the necessary skills to build a vessel that was to face the most terrible storm ever known.

Moreover, the days of Noah were days of *strong delusion*. In commenting on the days of Noah, Jesus passed over the wickedness of that age and underlined the ignorance of coming judgment that characterized the antediluvians, despite the fact that Noah had been preaching it for years. They "knew not," Jesus said, "until the flood came, and took them all away" (Matt. 24:38–39). They were blinded by their secular humanism, materialism, and occultism.

Then, too, the days of Noah were days of *some devotion*, for God never leaves Himself without a witness. The more degenerate the times, the more definite the testimony, both in terms of faithful preaching on the one hand and fulfilled prophecy on the other hand. Noah was a preacher (2 Peter 2:5) and Enoch was a prophet (Jude 14–15). A sample of his prophetic preaching is preserved in the book of Jude. Both bore witness to coming judgment. Enoch gave a prophetic name to his son, Methuselah—it means, "When he dies it [i.e., the flood] shall come." The death of Methuselah, incidentally, took place in the first month of the flood year.

Finally, the days of Noah were days of *sudden destruction*. "My Spirit shall not always strive with man," God said (Gen. 6:3). A date was set in heaven for the flood to begin. When it came in all its fury, chaos descended on the planet. Only eight people were saved—those who had believed God and accepted the invitation to take refuge in the ark. They were all members of Noah's family.

These features of Noah's day are all characteristics of our day. We live in a world in which evil people and seducers are waxing worse and worse, a world ripening fast for judgment. In light of all this, "What manner of persons ought [we] to be?" Peter asks (2 Peter 3:11).

Devotion 43

The Innkeeper of Bethlehem

Luke 2

It was known as Chimham's Inn, and it was close by Bethlehem. It had been there for a thousand years. The prophet Jeremiah knew about it in his day (Jer. 41:17). It was a well-known place and was about to become the most famous inn in the world.

Caesar Augustus had set the whole world in motion. From the Danube to the Nile, from the Euphrates to the Pillars of Hercules, people were on the move, driven by an imperial decree. It paid no heed to anyone's age or condition. It simply forced them to journey to their ancestral homes to be taxed. The carpenter of Nazareth and his wife were thus forced to go to Bethlehem.

Doubtless this journey was contrary to what they had planned with a child on the way. The journey must have been hard and tiring for Mary and an anxious time for her husband. They arrived in the little town of Bethlehem at last, the city of David; and there (as Micah had foretold some seven hundred years before) the Christ was born. Think of it! The Creator of the universe was born in a barn, of all places, with manure for carpeting, cobwebs for curtains, and bats to fly His honor guard.

There was no room for them in the inn. In the first place, when Joseph and Mary arrived, the innkeeper was busy. The place was packed to the doors. People were paying outrageous prices for a corner in which to spread a bedroll. All about the innkeeper, people were clamoring for food, for wine, for fodder for their camels, for water. The innkeeper and his helpers were rushed off their feet. Supplies had to be fetched from neighboring farms. The innkeeper had to be here, there, and everywhere, dealing with salesmen, keeping an eye on the kitchen, harrying the maids, taking in the cash, entertaining his guests.

Joseph was just another interruption, a Galilean peasant with a pregnant wife and a donkey! And he was from despised Nazareth, too, if the innkeeper were any judge of accents. "*No!* There is *no* room. *No room,* don't you understand? The place is full. You should have made reservations. I'm sorry about your wife, but that's your problem, not mine."

It is not too hard to picture Joseph, driven to it, perhaps, by desperation, turning on the innkeeper. "Look here, Mr. Innkeeper. I don't expect you to know who we are. I am Joseph, a direct descendant of David, through the line of Solomon. My wife is also a descendant of David through the collateral line of Nathan, Solomon's brother. The Child that is about to be born is rightful heir to David's usurped throne. You can't allow Him to be born on the street." We can imagine the innkeeper saying, "All right, use the cattle shed," and then going back to his work.

And thus it was that the Lord of glory arrived on planet Earth by way of a virgin's womb. He was born in a stable and laid in a manger. While people slept and angels sang and the innkeeper retired to his bed to snore his way through the miracle of miracles that took place that night in his stable, the Son of God became the Son of Man so that the children of men might become the children of God.

The innkeeper of Bethlehem has gone down in history. God kindly withholds his name. All we know about him was that he had no room for Jesus. Mind you, he had a perfectly good room in his inn he could have given to Jesus—his own. It was the best room in the inn, and he never thought of giving that up. What a sad way to be remembered—as the man who had no room for the Son of God.

SATAN'S POWER

LUKE 10:19

The word for total, absolute power in the New Testament is *dunamis* (from which we get our English word "dynamite"). Before the resurrection of Christ, Satan wielded this power. The Lord, for instance, spoke of "all the power [*dunamis*] of the enemy" (Luke 10:19).

In this age, however, Satan's power has been curbed. The kind of power (*dunamis*) Satan once had has now been given to the church. The Lord told His disciples: "Ye shall receive power [*dunamis*], after that the Holy Ghost is come upon you" (Acts 1:8). In writing to the church at Rome, Paul declared, "I am not ashamed of the gospel of Christ: for it is the power [*dunamis*] of God unto salvation to every one that believeth" (Rom. 1:16).

So, although Satan wields tremendous power, the fact remains that all his power is under restraint. The Holy Spirit restrains him, holds him back, and at times administers major setbacks to his plans by sending revival to the church. "Greater is he that is in you," the Bible says, "than he that is in the world" (1 John 4:4). Satan is no match for the Holy Spirit of God.

In this present age Satan's power is described by the word *exousia*. The word suggests delegated authority. At His return the Lord Jesus is going to put down all rule and authority (1 Cor. 15:24). Satan, today, is "the prince of the power [authority] of the air" (Eph. 2:2). As believers, we have been delivered from the power (authority) of darkness and have been translated into the kingdom of God's dear Son (Col. 1:13). Paul was commissioned to turn people from the power (authority) of Satan unto God (Acts 26:18). Jesus came to destroy the works of the Devil (1 John 3:8).

After the rapture of the church, Satan will receive back his *dunamis*; his ancient power, and that will enable him to bring in his agent, the

Antichrist. This ominous person's coming will be "after the working of Satan with all power [*dunamis*] and signs and lying wonders" (2 Thess. 2:9). His hour of triumph will be spectacular. He will succeed in bringing the whole world under his control. But his day will be short. The Lord, at His coming to reign, will put an end to Satan's long-sought, short-lived triumph on this earth.

"He must reign," Paul says of Christ (1 Cor. 15:25). Of course, He must! This world was the scene of His rejection, and it is going to be the scene of His glory and power. He will reign for a thousand years in righteousness on the very planet where He was cast out and crucified.

At the end of that reign, Satan, incarcerated in the Abyss for its entire period, will be released long enough to lead a final, massive revolt against Christ. Millions of people will be born in the millennial age. Large numbers of them will be born again and will become heirs of the kingdom. Countless others, however, will not be born again. They will long to indulge their natural lusts but will fear the long arm of the Lord. The psalmist tells us that the Lord will rule this planet with "a rod of iron" (Ps. 2:9). Satan will find these unregenerate malcontents willing tools for his final revolt. "Then cometh the end [*telos*, the very end]," Paul says (1 Cor. 15:24). Satan's revolt will be crushed. The world will be disintegrated and replaced by a new heaven and a new earth. The wicked dead of all the ages will be raised, judged, and banished to a lost eternity. All things will then come under Christ's control. Once all things are subdued by Christ, "then shall the Son also himself be subject unto him that put all things under him, that God may be all in all" ("everything to everyone" is the way it has been rendered; 1 Cor. 15:28). What a day of rejoicing that will be.

Devotion 45

THE LITTLE FLOCK

LUKE 12:32

F ear not, little flock; for it is your Father's good pleasure to give you
the kingdom."

The background of this statement is the parable of the rich fool
whose rosy prospects were all built upon a fatal delusion. All this prosperous farmer could think about was his bursting barns. He had "much
goods," it says (Luke 12:19). He thought also that he had "many years."
The poor fool. Little did he know that he would be dead before another
sunrise.

In contrast with this rich fool are the Lord's disciples, poor and weak
and in a hostile world but rich toward God. The Lord paints three pictures for them in less than a dozen and a half words.

There is a picture of a *little flock*, of no account in the world's scale of
values, but of vast importance in God's. A little flock! Not a herd, not
a swarm, not a pack, but a flock, and a *little* flock at that. God's people
never become an overwhelming majority in this world. David's brother
sneered: "With whom hast thou left those few sheep in the wilderness?"
(1 Sam. 17:28). Napoleon once said, "God is on the side of the big bat-
talions." Napoleon was a fool.

The world forgets the basic fact that the little flock it so despises is
God's little flock. The Lord Jesus appears in the Apocalypse as a little
lamb (Rev. 5:6), in appearance as a slain lamb. But let no one forget that
this little lamb has seven horns (omnipotence) and seven eyes (omniscience) and that Satan's great red dragon is no match for Him. God
stopped Napoleon with snowflake after snowflake after snowflake, until
his conquering armies ground to a halt, surrounded by snowflakes and
frozen with the cold.

Then there is a picture of *a loving father*. "Fear not, little flock; for it is
your *Father's* good pleasure to give you the kingdom." God is referred to

as a Father only about four or five times in the entire Old Testament. He was known by many mighty and magnificent names, but none of them compared with this new name Jesus brought with Him to earth— "Father!" God is "our Father," He said. In the Lord's incomparable twin parable of the prodigal and his elder brother, the name "father" occurs twelve times (Luke 15:11–32). So the picture of a flock is replaced now by the picture of a family. The God and Father of our Lord Jesus Christ is now our *God* and Father. Moreover it is His good pleasure to provide and protect and plan, and all for our present and eternal bliss.

Finally, there is a picture of *a lofty future*. "It is your Father's good pleasure to give you the kingdom." It is a long way from the pasture to the palace. David made it. So shall we.

It has always been God's purpose to establish a kingdom in this world. When He created Adam, He gave him "dominion" (Gen. 1:26). Throughout the Old Testament period, God pursued that purpose. Israel's first attempt to establish a monarchy was disastrous. They chose a king after their own, rebellious hearts. Then David came, "a man after God's own heart." Had it not been for the disastrous Bathsheba affair, David might well have conquered all the Promised Land, from the Nile to the Euphrates. The long apostasy-riddled history of the earthly kingdom climaxed in the fall of both Israel and Judah. The monarchy became the dependency, and the land fell under foreign rule.

Then Jesus came. John the Baptist proclaimed Him as the long-awaited Messiah. Had the Jewish people accepted Him, the empire of Christ would have spread throughout the world. They rejected Him. "We have no king but Caesar," they said to Pontius Pilate (John 19:15). Pilate knew better. He wrote his own title for the cross: "This is Jesus of Nazareth the King of the Jews."

During this present age, God's kingdom purposes are in abeyance. He is building a church, and His kingdom is essentially spiritual in nature (John 3:3, 5–8).

But the King is coming back. The kingdom will come. Jesus will reign. And when He does enter into His kingdom, so shall we. It is the Father's good pleasure to guarantee that.

Devotion 46

THE UNSEEN WORLD

LUKE 16

There is a vocabulary of half a dozen words in the Greek text of the Bible to depict for us various facts about the underworld. First, there is the word *hades* and its equivalent Hebrew word *sheol*. The basic idea behind the word *sheol* is "the grave" (as distinguished from "a grave," a mere burying place). The word occurs sixty-five times in the Old Testament. The word *hades*, which occurs eleven times in the New Testament, means "the unseen." Both *sheol* and *hades* refer to the abode of the dead, and both give the impression of it being in a downward direction. Samuel, for instance, castigated King Saul for bringing him "up" when the king sought help from the witch of Endor (I Sam. 28:15). At death, the Lord Jesus "descended" into the lower parts of the earth (Eph. 4:9–10).

The incident of the rich man and Lazarus (Luke 16) tells us much about hades. In Jesus' day, it was in two sections divided by a great gulf. The rich man was on one side in a place of torment. Lazarus was on the other side. He had been carried by the angels to "Abraham's bosom," a Hebrew idiom for a place of rest, fellowship, and happiness. The rich man was consciously lost. He was in agony, and he was anxious for his lost brothers. He learned he was beyond help or hope. Abraham's side of the gulf was known as "paradise," a word that suggests a park-like abode of bliss (Luke 23:43).

At the time of Christ's ascension, the paradise section of hades seems to have been moved to a different place. Paul was "caught up" to it (2 Cor. 12:4) and experienced things that were beyond description. In one way they were of a material nature because Paul thought himself to be still "in the body" (v. 3). In another way they were of a mystical nature because he thought himself to be "out of the body." From then on, Paul had a strong desire to return to that place and to be with Christ, which he said was "far better." The expression can be rendered "far, far better." The use of the superlative emphasizes the joy that awaits us there (Phil. 1:23).

Another word is *Gehenna*. This word refers to the final abode of the wicked dead. It is called "the lake of fire" at the end of the Apocalypse (Rev. 20:14). The Greek word is a transliteration of the Hebrew word for "the valley of Hinnom," where apostate Jews sacrificed their children to idols on the red-hot lap of Molech (1 Kings 11:7). King Josiah put an end to the practice. The site itself was a place where three valleys united south of Jerusalem. In Jesus' day, it was the city garbage dump, and fires burned there continually consuming the dross. It became a synonym and type of hell with its unquenchable fire (Mark 9:43–48).

At the great white throne judgment, death and hades will be emptied into the lake of fire as the bodies and souls of the wicked dead are reunited and cast into hell itself (Rev. 20:14).

The Hebrew word for "heaven" comes from a root word that is the usual word for the sky. The corresponding Greek word became the name for God's home. The idea of heaven occurs often in the New Testament. We are to pray, for instance, to "our Father which art in heaven" (Matt. 6:9). John, in the Apocalypse, saw "a door . . . opened in heaven" (4:1). Heaven is a real place. Jesus said it contains many mansions (John 14:2). The description given of the celestial city (Rev. 4–5; 21–22) gives us our best impression of what heaven will be like. We shall dwell in heaven in our resurrection bodies in "joy unspeakable and full of glory" (1 Peter 1:8).

The word *tartarus* is used only by Peter, and it refers to the prison house of the worst of the fallen angels (2 Peter 2:4). These beings not only supported Satan in his initial rebellion, but they also lusted after human women and helped debauch the world of Noah's day (Gen. 6:4; Jude 6–7).

There is one other word, *abussos* (the Abyss), often translated "bottomless pit." It is the place where evil spirits of great malevolence and power are incarcerated for now (Rev. 9:1–12) and where Satan will be imprisoned during the millennium (Rev. 20:1–3).

The unseen world is real. We need to make sure we belong to the Lord Jesus who has the keys of death and hades and who alone is the way to heaven. "No man cometh unto the Father, but by me," He says (John 14:6).

Devotion 47

THE EMMAUS ROAD

LUKE 24:13-33

There they go, two of the Lord's disciples. Their backs are toward Jerusalem, the city that historically had stoned the prophets and martyred God's ministers and but lately had murdered its Messiah. Their faces are toward the village of Emmaus.

It was a seven-mile hike into the country. These sad disciples walked with feet of lead, as heavy as their heavy hearts. And, of course, they talked together. Enough things had happened in Jerusalem over the past few days to keep them talking for a very long time. The wonder-working Jesus had come riding into the city, hailed by the people as the very Messiah Himself. The religious establishment, however, was determined to put Him to death. They had bought Judas, browbeaten Pilate, and manipulated the mob. They had hounded Jesus of Nazareth to the cross and to His death. Now, three days later, it was evidently all over, and they were going home talking about these things as they walked.

Then Jesus came up alongside them, but they did not know it was He. They thought He was just a fellow traveler. We get three glimpses of these disciples on that never-to-be-forgotten Emmaus road.

How mistaken they were. This stranger, who had joined them, seemed to them to be astoundingly ignorant of the tremendous events that had stirred the whole country for weeks. "Art thou only a stranger in Jerusalem, and hast not known the things which are come to pass there in these days?" they said (Luke 24:18).

What a question! He was no stranger in Jerusalem. He had watched over its history for two thousand years. Indeed, if the truth were told, it was His city. As for the recent events that had taken place there, well He knew more about those things than they did because they had all happened to *Him!* He had scars on his back and wounds in his hands and feet and side to prove it. These two Emmaus disciples walked six or seven miles with Jesus and didn't know it was He Himself who talked to them. How often have we failed to recognize Him too?

We note, too, *how miserable they were.* It was patently obvious to Jesus that these disciples were discouraged, totally demoralized, and completely downcast. They spilled it all out, the sad story of their crucified hopes. "We trusted that it had been he which should have redeemed Israel," they said (v. 21). What had He been doing on the cross if He hadn't been providing redemption for Israel—and for all mankind? Redemption involves paying a price for something of great value, often pawned for little more than a song. And what a price He had paid! The price of our redemption was His precious blood poured out in agony on the cross. They did not understand that. No wonder misery had been their shadow on that long walk to Emmaus.

Finally, *how moved they were.* The stranger began to talk. He gave them a Bible survey, reviewing for them all that the prophets had written and showing them in all the Scriptures the things concerning Himself. He talked to them about the covering God had provided for fallen, naked Adam and Eve. He talked about Noah and his ark, about Joseph, about the Passover and the offerings, and about Isaiah 53 and Psalms 22 and 69.

Their hearts burned. And it was this inspired exegesis of the Bible that did it! Then suddenly the journey was over. They were home! They asked Him in and showed Him to His place at the table. It seemed only natural to ask Him to give thanks for the food, so He blessed and broke the bread. And they saw His hands! And He was gone! They hurried back to Jerusalem with songs. *He was alive!* And they arrived in the upper room just in time to see Him again!

He is still at it—opening unto us the Scriptures, making our hearts burn within us, giving us glimpses of Himself. Blessed be His name!

Devotion 48

"AND THE WORD WAS MADE FLESH"

JOHN 1:14

A nd the Word was made flesh, and dwelt among us, (and we beheld his glory, the glory as of the only begotten of the Father,) full of grace and truth."

At once our attention is drawn to the *Godhead* and the mystery of Jesus' person. "God is a spirit," Jesus told the woman at the well (John 4:24). As the second person of the Godhead, so was He; but He was also "made flesh." That is to say, He assumed humanity and inhabited a body of flesh and blood. Paul expresses the awesomeness of that. He says, "In him dwelleth all the fulness of the Godhead bodily" (Col. 2:9).

"In the beginning," John explains, "was the Word" (John 1:1). That does not refer to a *start* but a *state*. We go back to the beginning of things, and He was there.

"And the Word was God," John continues. The Word was "with God," a separate person within the Godhead. The reference is to His essential deity. The verb "was" is not in the past tense but in the imperfect tense.

"The same was in the beginning with God," John adds, taking us back before the creation. "All things were made by him," he declares, naming Him as the Creator of the entire universe (vv. 2–3).

And, finally, we come to this: "The Word was made flesh." God became *Man*. There now lives a *Man* who is God. Paul says, "Being in the form of God, [he] thought it not robbery to be equal with God." However, He "took upon him the form of a servant." He was "made in the likeness of men." And He was "found in fashion as a man" (Phil. 2:6–8). There are enough mysteries there to occupy us for all eternity.

John now turns to the Lord's *grace*. He came and dwelt among us. The word he used means that He "pitched His tent" among us, or, literally, He "tabernacled" among us. The very word takes us back a millennium and a half to the days of Moses. For God told Moses He had decided to come down to earth and live with His people. What grace! He came from the mansions of glory, from a rainbow-circled throne. Countless angels in robes of light hung upon His words and rushed to do His will. Yet down to earth He came to "tabernacle" with people, to dwell in a tent in the midst of His pilgrim people, all the way from Sinai to the Promised Land. Isn't that just like Him?

Finally, we catch a glimpse of His *glory*. There was nothing beautiful about the outside covering of the Old Testament tabernacle, but inside it was all gleaming gold, brilliant color, and costly fabric—all ablaze with the light of another world.

Similarly, the glory of the Lord Jesus was a hidden glory. His *majestic* glory, the glory He had with His Father before the world began, was rarely seen. He had emptied Himself of that. John caught just a glimpse of it at the transfiguration (Matt. 17:1–2). His *moral* glory was evident to all who had eyes to see. John saw it and describes it as the "glory as of the only begotten of the Father, . . . full of grace and truth" (John 1:14). Grace is the overflow of God's *love*. Truth is the substance of God's *Law*. Both were in perfect balance in Christ. For those who had eyes to see and ears to hear, that glory was their foretaste of heaven. Such is our Lord and our God.

Devotion 49

"YE MUST BE BORN AGAIN"

JOHN 3

The words shook Nicodemus to the core of his being. They cut through his opening *pleasantries* in which he conceded that God was with the young prophet from Nazareth. The words cut through his conscientious *philanthropies*—his tithes, his offerings, his contributions to the poor. The words shattered his religious *priorities*—fasting, keeping the law, working his way to heaven. "Except a man be born again," Jesus declared, "he cannot see the kingdom of God" (John 3:3).

But, first, let us look at *the man*. Nicodemus was rich. His contribution to the burial of Christ, for instance, was a hundred pounds of costly spices, a fortune, far beyond anything an ordinary workingman could afford (19:39).

He was *respected* as "a ruler of the Jews" (3:1), a member of the Sanhedrin, the chief governing body of the nation.

He was *religious*, being a member of the sect of the Pharisees, fanatics for the letter of the Law. "Surely," he said to himself, "if any man deserves to go to heaven, I do." His credentials were impeccable. He had spent his whole life climbing the religious ladder. Now, belatedly, he discovered it was leaning against the wrong wall. Such was the man, the very finest product of self-righteous religion.

What troubled him was *the message*. Jesus had just informed him that what he needed was a new birth, a new beginning altogether. Curiously enough, religious though he was, the Lord's words struck an unsuspected responsive chord. He did not say, "*Why?*" He said, "*How?*" Nicodemus said, "How can a man be born when he is old?" (v. 4). Can we not detect a note of longing in those words? Nicodemus was an honest man. He knew how far short he had come of the glory of God. All his almsgiving and zeal for the Law and religious observances notwithstanding, he knew that something was missing. His goodness was only relative goodness. He compared favorably when he measured himself alongside people like the publican, the harlot, and the thief, but God demanded *absolute* goodness. Yes, indeed! To be born again, to become as an innocent babe—that was it! But how?

Which brings us to *the message*. Nicodemus needed to be "born of water and of the Spirit" (v. 5). The Lord's reference to water clearly pointed to the well-known baptism of John, a baptism of *repentance*. Nicodemus had not submitted to that baptism. The Pharisees, as a group, had officially rejected both John and his baptism. They wrapped their religious robes about them and shuddered at the thought of taking their place in the water as *sinners*. Not for a single moment could they imagine themselves taking their place in the line to confess their need for repentance and to submit to being baptized by John.

The Lord's references to the baptism of the Spirit underlined Nicodemus's need to be *regenerated*, to be born again by the Holy Spirit. What he needed was new life, spiritual life. He needed to receive the life of God which could be imparted only by the Holy Spirit and only to a humble, repentant man. So there was the message.

Finally, there was *the method*. "But how," asked the Pharisee, "can a man enter into his mother's womb and be reborn?" The Lord explained: "As Moses lifted up the serpent in the wilderness [a reference to an Old Testament incident well known to Nicodemus], even so must the Son of man be lifted up [a reference to the Lord's coming crucifixion]" (v. 14). Nicodemus saw it at once.

In the Old Testament story (Num. 21), the unbelieving Israelites in the wilderness had been bitten by serpents. There was no medical remedy, and they were dying in droves. At God's command, Moses made a brass serpent and fastened it to a pole. Then he lifted it up for all to see. "Look, and live!" he said. That was all it took—a look of faith. No good works were required, no religious ceremony, no supposed personal merit—just a look! That was the story, and here was its meaning: Jesus would be lifted up as the Sin-Bearer. He would be "made sin." All that was needed to live forever was to look in simple faith to Him. A few short years later, Nicodemus saw Christ lifted up on the cross. And that was it! He looked! He lived! He was born again.

MARTHA, MARY, AND LAZARUS

JOHN 12:1–9

Martha was a *worker*. The death, burial, and resurrection of Lazarus profoundly changed her attitude toward serving the Lord and His people. Before, she had been critical of Mary. No longer! She had buried her touchiness in the grave of Lazarus. Now she served as one standing on resurrection ground. Mary was a *worshiper*. She was always at Jesus' feet, listening attentively to the Lord's words. She had one prized possession, a flask of very expensive perfume. Perhaps she had kept it in her room for the day of her wedding or, failing that, the day of her burial. Listening to Jesus changed her mind. It dawned on her that Jesus was soon going to die. He would need ointment for His burying. She said nothing but, from then on, treasured up that costly perfume for *Him*. Doubtless she had been put under considerable pressure by Martha to give it for the burying of Lazarus. She refused, much as she loved her brother. She kept it, Jesus said, "against the day of my burying hath she kept this" (John 12:7).

Then something else took hold of her heart. At the time the Lord raised Lazarus, He declared Himself to be "the resurrection, and the life" (John 11:25). Mary seized on that. "So," she said to herself, "He'll really not need this ointment for His *burying* after all. He's going to rise again. I'll not wait until He's dead. The next time He comes, I'll give it to Him then." And so she did.

Lazarus, of course, was a *witness*. He had been a believer for some time, one of Jesus' closest friends. His home had long been a gathering place for those who loved the Lord. Everyone knew that. But the fact that he was a believer did not much interest people. Nobody beat a path to his door to see him just because he was a believer.

But look at them now. We read, "Much people of the Jews . . . came . . . that they might see Lazarus . . . whom [Jesus] had raised from the dead" (v. 9). They are coming in droves. What made the difference? Resurrection! There is something wonderfully attractive about someone living a resurrected life.

Suppose we were to ask Lazarus: "What is the secret of this new life of yours?" He would say: "I was always a devout believer, you know. But one day I died. I died to my family, to my career, to my opinions—to everything. I was very dead indeed. You don't expect much from a dead man. Martha knew I was dead. 'By this time he stinketh,' she said. She was right. All you can do with a dead man is bury him.

"Then Jesus came. I had come to an utter end of myself. Jesus gave me new life—resurrection life. I am not the same Lazarus you used to know. That Lazarus died. Now 'I live, yet not I but Christ liveth in me.' I am a witness to what Christ can do with a dead man. I am a living epistle, known and read of all men. I am not *trying* to be a witness, you understand. I don't go out knocking on doors. I don't hand out tracts. I didn't take a course on soul winning. I just live a resurrected life. That's all. God does the rest."

And the people came. One suspects they would still come if we would live resurrected lives.

Devotion 51

MARY MAGDALENE AND THE RESURRECTION

JOHN 20:1-2, 11-18

She had already been to the tomb and found it open and empty, and she had found Peter and John and told them the tale. They left her standing in a cloud of dust as they raced each other to the tomb. Slowly she made her way back, drawn as by a magnet to that opened sepulcher.

We note her *distress*. There had been some coming and going; but all that was past, and now Mary stood there alone. "She stood without at the sepulchre weeping," John says (John 20:11). The word for "weeping," the same one used of Mary of Bethany when she went to meet Jesus at Lazarus's tomb, literally means "to wail." Mary of Magdala was desolated. Her only thought was that someone had broken into the tomb and stolen the body. Who could have done such a thing? Perhaps it was the Sanhedrin, determined to wreak their wrath on the human clay of the Christ of God by dumping the body in a criminal's grave or, worse still, in the fires of the Valley of Gehenna. She wept.

We note also her *discovery*. She did what John had done. She stooped down to peer inside the tomb. And, behold, it was empty no more! Two angels had come, and one was sitting where the head had been and the other where the feet had been. Perhaps it was Gabriel, the messenger angel, and Michael, the martial angel.

By this time all Jerusalem and all Judea should have been crowding to that empty tomb to view the evidence that it bore to a resurrected Christ. The only ones who came were two messengers from another world, and one lone, weeping woman from this one.

We note next her *disinterest*. She turned her back on the angels. It was not angels she wanted; it was Jesus. Her disinterest in them must have astonished them. Usually when they appeared, people trembled, stood and stared, or fell flat on the ground. No one had ever ignored them before.

And, standing there in the shadows, delighted at such single-hearted love, was Jesus. For no sooner did Mary turn from the angels than she saw Him.

Note, also, her *despair.* She did not recognize the One who now caught and held her eye. She supposed He was the gardener. He was, of course! He it was, long centuries before, who had planted a garden eastward in Eden as a home for Adam and Eve. "Are you the one who has taken the body?" she said. "Please tell me where He is. I want Him. I love Him. I'll take Him away." There was not much logic in that—but there was a whole lot of love.

Finally we see her *delight.* The Lord could contain Himself no longer. Here was love stronger than death, love that many waters could not quench. "Mary!" He said. "Master!" she replied. One word, answered by one word. Often love needs no words. Here two words said it all: "Mary!" "Master!"

She would have clung to Him, but He said, "Touch Me not. There are things I have to do. I must go to My Father. And there are things you have to do. You must go and tell My disciples I am alive and will meet them soon in Galilee."

And so she did, and thus became the first evangelist of the gospel age.

Devotion 52

JOHN AND THE RESURRECTION

JOHN 20:1-10

John took his pen in hand to write his gospel toward the end of the first century. The church was under attack—persecution from without, perversion from within. Apostasy was entrenched in high places. The third generation was now in charge, and truth was put up for sale.

In the first generation of a movement, *conviction* rules. Truth, dearly bought, is defended to the death. In the second generation, conviction degenerates into *belief*. People raised in the great truths they have been taught believe them and will argue for them; but the passion and the power has gone. In the third generation, belief becomes *opinion*, and opinions easily can be changed. John wrote for this perilous third generation, which was busy selling its birthright for a mess of this world's pottage. He took his readers back to the beginning.

It was all as fresh and as vivid in his mind as though it were yesterday. His thoughts flew back to the wonderful years he had spent in the company of Jesus. He would write about them. The skeptics, liberals, and Gnostics could be silenced by John in three words: "I was there!" He would take that careless third generation back to where it all began. John, of course, realized that the world itself could not contain the books that he could have written about Jesus. So he concentrated on a few special signs and sayings of Jesus. And, of course, he had some important things to say about the resurrection, the cornerstone of our faith.

So far as John was concerned, his recollection of all the wonderful happenings of the resurrection day began with a woman. Her love for Jesus (living or dead) drove her from her bed before the break of day. She must have been a brave woman. She was not afraid of the dark, or of the guard, or of being alone in a cemetery. Perfect love had cast out all her fear. But there was no guard! The stone was rolled away! The tomb was empty! She fled on winged feet to tell John.

So it was, still early in the morning, that John and Peter came to see for themselves. And this is what John saw—grave clothes. They spoke volumes to him.

When burying their dead, the Jews took linen cloths and made bandages of them, tearing them into long strips—fine linen for the rich, old rags for the poor. Then they took large quantities of myrrh and aloes. They saturated the linen strips with liquid spices and wound them round and round the body. As they dried, these linen strips hardened and formed a rigid casing around the body.

John saw the bandages lying in the tomb stiff, like a tube. He saw the napkin, folded and lying apart. He could see the hole in the mummy wrapping where the body once had been. There was a space between the head-shaped napkin and the tube-shaped body clothes, where the neck should have been. But there was nothing there but empty space. The turban-shaped head napkin was empty. The tubular-shaped body wrappings, stark and stiff like a canister, were empty. There could be only one explanation. *Christ had risen right through the grave clothes.* He was gone! The grave clothes remained. John was convinced. The Lord was risen indeed.

Devotion 53

THOMAS AND THE RESURRECTION

JOHN 20:24-29

It was not so much the *mind* of Thomas that had to be captured before he could believe in the resurrection. With John it was a matter of the mind. Nor was it so much a matter of the *heart* as it was with Mary. With Thomas it was a matter of the *will*. "I *will* not believe!" he said. Those were his very own words.

But let us back up. The day of the resurrection was over. What a day it had been! We can imagine the confusion and consternation that reigned in the ranks of God's enemies. What, we wonder, did Pilate say to his wife when news of Christ's resurrection came filtering in? And there could not have been much mocking now by Herod and his men of war. As for Caiaphas and his gang of renegade priests, well might they stare at one another in silent dismay. It was not that they took it lying down, however. It was in keeping with their determined unbelief that they should forge and foist a lie upon the world. Just the same, the truth was that Jesus was alive from the dead. Well may they tremble in their secret souls. What kind of vengeance would He deal out to them?

But in that blessed upper room, it had been a foretaste of glory. Jesus had come in through the wall! He had shown the disciples His hands and His side. He had sat down and eaten a meal. Then He had vanished from their sight. He was *alive*—alive to die no more! Whether they could see Him or not, He was alive!

And poor Thomas had not been there! Doubtless he had his excuses—"That upper room is a dangerous place just now," he might have said to himself. "And the meetings are boring these days. No doubt Simon Peter will be throwing his weight around. Besides, it looks like rain!" In the end he went to the gathering but, when he did finally show up, it was all over. He'd missed it! The others tried to tell him that Jesus had come! He dug in his heels. "I will not believe," he said. "I want proof, hard, tangible proof."

But we know this: Thomas was there the next Sunday! Perhaps he remembered the simple rule for gathering that Jesus had laid down— "Where two or three are gathered together in my name, there am I in the midst of them" (Matt. 18:20). He made up his mind to be there.

And it happened again, just as before. All of a sudden, Jesus was there in their midst. And there was Thomas in his usual seat. Up to the startling moment of truth we can picture the stubborn set of his shoulders, the scornful look on his face, the fixed jut of his jaw.

But that jaw dropped in a hurry. For there was Jesus smiling at him across the room. "Thomas," He said, "come over here. Look at the nail prints if that's what it takes. Give me your hand. Come and put it into my side."

"My Lord and my God!" cried Thomas, his will broken and his heart broken too. "My Lord!" That put Jesus on the throne of his heart. "My God!" That put Jesus on the throne of the universe.

"Well, Thomas," Jesus said, "you have seen and believed. But blessed are those who have not seen, and yet have believed." Surely the Lord had us in mind. We have not seen—but we have believed. "Blessed art thou!" He says, "Blessed art thou."

PETER AND THE RESURRECTION

JOHN 21

With John, the impact of the resurrection was a matter of the mind. With Mary Magdalene, it was an affair of the heart. With Thomas, it was a question of the will. But with Peter, it was a matter of the conscience.

Peter had failed worse than any of the disciples. He had boasted of his superior loyalty to the Lord and then had denied Him with oaths and curses. The Lord already had dealt with Peter privately. Now, by the shore of Galilee, He deals with Peter publicly. First, we see the Lord *recalling Peter's failure*. Everything about the scene was intended to quicken Peter's conscience. For instance, there was the fire of coals to remind him of the courtyard of the high priest's palace. There was the use of his old name—"Simon, son of Jonas." There was the thrice repeated challenge, "Lovest thou me?" recalling Peter's three denials. There was the question about the fish, recalling that Jesus had called Peter to be "a fisher of men" and that Peter apparently had gone back to his old fishing trade. All these things recalled Peter's failure.

We also see Jesus *rekindling Peter's fervor*. The Lord did hot harp on the past. He never torments us with our failure. He deals with it, once and for all, so that it will never have to be raised again.

We are all familiar with the play here on the two words for love. "Do you *love* me, Peter?" the Lord said. "Do you love me with that highest, holiest form of love, with the love that is divine and deathless, spiritual and pure?"

Peter answered cautiously, conscious of his terrible fall: "Lord, You know I have a deep affection for You—a *brotherly* love for You."

"Do you love me, Peter?" the Lord said again, using the same high word for love as before. "Lord," said Peter, "You know I am very fond of You—I have a *brotherly* love for You."

Then the question was put to him again, only this time the Lord used Peter's word: "Are you fond of me?" He asked. Peter was broken. "Lord, You know. You know I can never love You the way You love me. But You know my heart. You know I have a *brotherly* love for You—a warm, and human kind of love."

Then we see the Lord *reshaping Peter's future.* "Then feed my lambs," Jesus said. "Feed my sheep. Feed the flock of God. Peter, I have already given you an evangelistic ministry. I have called you to be a fisher of men. Now I am also going to give you a pastoral ministry. I want you to take care of the flock of God.

"Oh, and by the way, Peter, there's something more. I not only want to draw your attention to the *fish* and to the *flock.* I also want to draw your attention to the *foe.* I told you once before that Satan desired to have you to sift you as wheat. Well, he still wants you. He will attack you when you are old. You will be put to death for me. You will be crucified. And this time, Peter, there will be no fall. I have recalled your failure and I have rekindled your fervor for one reason only—so that I can reshape your future."

That is ever His goal.

Devotion 55

GO FORWARD

ACTS 7:20–37

Moses was all too familiar with the atmosphere of Pharaoh's court. He had been raised in it and was "learned in all the wisdom of the Egyptians" (Acts 7:22). The scholars who took Moses in hand, at the request of Pharaoh's daughter, had their work cut out for them, for what they taught was contrary to what his people taught. When he came to manhood, Moses rejected the wisdom, the wealth, and the ways of Egypt. He was not impressed by a later Pharaoh's scornful, "I know not the LORD" (Exod. 5:2). Pharaoh thought he was a God, Ra, the incarnation of the sun. But if Pharaoh did not know the Lord, Moses did. And that was the difference between them. Moses knew God; therefore, Pharaoh was no match for him. By the time Moses was finished with him, having visited him with plague after plague and having left him at last with a dead child in every Egyptian home, Pharaoh was terrified of both Moses and his God. At least he was terrified for twenty-four hours or so.

The Pharaoh of Moses' day was the great, red dragon of the Nile. He was controlled by "the spirit that now worketh in the children of disobedience" (Eph. 2:2), and Pharaoh had his army and thousands of men to march at his word. Moses had a little lamb, a Passover lamb. The various miracles of Moses did not bring about Israel's release. They only made the monarch mad. He was broken at last by means of the death of the lamb. Its blood was shed, and it was roasted with fire, making a feast for the people of God.

The people believed God, and some three million of them were saved in one spectacular night. Israel was "a nation born in a day." The emancipated people marched out of Egypt by the thousands, carrying with them a sizable share of the wealth of the land. The sight and sound of them disappearing in the distance was too much for the Egyptian king. He reacted against his decision to let them go. He mobilized his men!

He marched after them! He would bring them back! He would make them pay! The fools were heading for the sea! He would trap them there with his soldiers behind and the Red Sea before.

All too soon Pharaoh had forgotten about God. The intended military move of encirclement, followed by a swift cavalry charge, was halted by a miracle, as though Pharaoh had not had more than enough of miracles. The Shechinah glory cloud, which had been leading Israel, now moved to the rear and stood between the Egyptians and their prey. The fiery, cloudy pillar was the visible token that God was on Israel's side. To get at the people, the Egyptian cavalry would first need to get past God Himself. And Pharaoh, puppet god of Egypt as he imagined himself to be, was no match for the true and living God.

"Go forward!" Those were God's words to His people. But how? Then it happened. A wide way opened up through the sea, and seizing their opportunity they crossed over. The foolhardy Egyptians seized what looked like a golden opportunity to overwhelm the fleeing Hebrews. The Shechinah pillar stood aside, making way for the Egyptians to march. The cavalry troops of the Egyptian army lashed their horses. The chariots and horsemen surged into the gap between the piled-up seas. Then disaster struck them. The wheels fell off their chariots. The waters suddenly returned. The Egyptians perished in the sea.

The pathway to Canaan now opened before the victorious Israelites. They followed the guiding pillar. It led them along a grand highway— separation, song, security, sanctification!

First there was *separation.* The water of the Red Sea came between the Hebrews and their old way of life. Next there was *song.* "Thus the LORD saved Israel," we read (Exod. 14:30). "Then sang Moses and the children of Israel" (15:1). *Security* followed as a matter of course—their every need was met by miracle after miracle: bread from heaven, water from the riven rock, victory over Amalek! Then, finally, there was *sanctification.* The redeemed Israelites were brought to Sinai and taught how to order their lives. Moreover, God Himself came down and pitched His tent in the midst of His own, to walk with them, and talk with them, and treat them like no other nation on earth. All these blessings were heaped up for them along the wilderness way, all this and Canaan too!

When God says, "Go forward," it is always best to obey.

Devotion 56

MUCH MORE

"Much more!" says Paul. He says it five times in a row. Behind the statement can be seen the shadow of the Old Testament trespass offering. Before the transgressor could offer his trespass offering, he had to pay fully whatever damage he had done, *plus* a penalty of an additional twenty percent (Lev. 5:16). Thus the wronged party actually became the gainer!

As a result of man's sin and God's salvation, we become the gainers. Adam might have lived in Eden in sinless perfection forever, but his posterity would have remained children of Adam. Now they get much more; they become children of God.

Moreover, God becomes the gainer. God could demonstrate His wisdom and His power in creation, but it was Calvary that gave Him a platform on which to demonstrate His love. As the old hymn puts it:

> God is love I surely know
> In the Savior's depths of woe.[1]

Paul shows us, with his five "much mores," five ways God has been able to demonstrate His love because of Calvary and thus become the gainer. We stand in awe of His wisdom and His power. We are overwhelmed by His love.

First, we look at *His love and His government*: "God commendeth His love toward us, in that, while we were yet sinners, Christ died for us. *Much more* then, being now justified by his blood, we shall be saved from wrath through him" (Rom. 5:8–9). Think for a moment of that word "justified." The Law can *forgive* a guilty person, but it cannot *justify* the

---

1. "Oh, My Savior Crucified," *Hymns for the Little Flock*, 1881.

person. To be forgiven, we must plead "guilty." To be justified means we are declared "not guilty." The best God's government—based only on His Law—can offer the sinner is a *fair trial* or a *free pardon*. The death of Christ at Calvary enables God to declare me justified—just as if I'd never sinned. Justification puts us beyond the reach of God's wrath. But at what a cost!

We think next of *His love and His goodness*: "For if, when we were enemies, we were reconciled to God by the death of his Son, *much more*, being reconciled, we shall be saved by his life" (Rom. 5:10). The Lord's goodness is absolute goodness, not relative goodness. It qualified Him to die on our behalf. He was like the Old Testament sacrificial lamb, without spot or blemish. Christ died so that we could escape the penalty of sin. But there is much more. He who gave His life for me to save me from the penalty of sin now gives His life to me, so that I can escape the power of sin.

Next, we contemplate *His love and His gift*: "But not as the offence, so also is the free gift. For if through the offence of one many be dead, *much more* the grace of God, and the gift by grace, which is by one man, Jesus Christ, hath abounded unto many" (Rom. 5:15). The first Adam bequeathed death on his children. That was his gift to us. God's gift is "eternal life through Jesus Christ our Lord" (Rom. 6:23). God in His superlative love does not just give us back natural life; He gives eternal life.

We think too of *His love and His glory*: "For if by one man's offence death reigned by one; *much more* they which receive abundance of grace and of the gift of righteousness shall reign in life by one, Jesus Christ" (Rom. 5:17). Again, God demonstrates the superlative nature of His love. We, who were once rebels, are now destined for the throne, to be seated with Christ in the highest heaven, above principalities and powers and every name that is named, not only in this life, but also in the life to come. We will reign with Him on high!

Finally, we think of *his love and his grace*: "But where sin abounded, grace did much more abound" (Rom. 5:20). Well might we sing the words of John Newton's hymn "Amazing Grace":

Amazing grace! how sweet the sound
That saved a wretch like me!
I once was lost, but now am found,
Was blind, but now I see.[2]

So, then, Calvary is the stage upon which God demonstrates His love. And we, the objects of that love, will be exhibited eternally as its trophies, to the admiration and wonder of all the angel throng.

2. John Newton, "Amazing Grace," 1779.

Devotion 57

A VERY REAL PROBLEM

ROMANS 7

There are three people in Romans 7. There is the *spiritual person* (vv. 1–6), the one who, "married to another," brings forth "fruit unto God." There is the *natural person*—Paul as he was in his unregenerate days (vv. 7–13—all the verbs here are in the past tense). Finally, there is the *carnal person* (vv. 14–25), the "wretched man" who knows the theology of the victorious life but is unable to make it work in practice. Paul brings his keen mind to bear on this problem, a mind in tune with the Holy Spirit.

First, he goes back to his unregenerate days. He reviews his career as a doomed sinner. He was condemned by the Law. In those days, he had tried by his own efforts at keeping God's Law to produce a standard of behavior God could accept, only to discover that the Law did four things that were against him.

The Law *revealed* sin. Paul said, "I had not known sin, but by the law . . . I had not known lust, except the law had said, Thou shalt not covet" (v. 7). He could run his eye down the list of the Ten Commandments and claim to have kept the first nine. The tenth commandment said, "Thou shalt have no evil desire," and that one slew him. And he knew it.

The Law *revived* sin. "When the commandment came, sin revived, and I died," Paul said (v. 9). How true that is! We see a sign that reads: "Keep off the grass" or "Don't touch." Before we see the sign, we have no thought of doing either one or the other. But when we see the forbidding sign, that is the very thing we want to do!

The Law *rewards* sin. It does not reward us for keeping its commandments because we are supposed to do that. The Law of God expects us to do what it says. It rewards us with punishment when we break its decrees. It is a stern taskmaster. It does not bend the rules.

Finally, the Law *rebukes* sin. The Law is "holy, and just, and good," Paul says (v. 12). Moreover, it makes sin "exceeding sinful" (v. 13) because, in the last analysis, all sin is high treason against God.

So there he was, a natural man, a *doomed sinner, condemned by the Law,* and unable to meet even heaven's minimum demands.

Now Paul reviews his career as a *defeated saint, conquered by lust.* Again he dissects his behavior. He comes up with four spiritual laws.

First, there is *the Law of Sinai.* That Law, the Law of God, pointed him heavenward and made it clear to him that God demands perfection, not only in keeping the letter of the Law, but also in keeping the spirit of the Law as expounded in the Sermon on the Mount.

There is also *the law of sin*—"I find then a law," says Paul, "that, when I would do good, evil is present with me" (v. 21). The law of sin pulled him downward. These two laws tore him apart. But there was more.

There is what Paul calls *"the law of my mind"* (v. 23). With his mind he consented unto the Law that it was good. His mind paid tribute to God's Law. He agreed that he should live the way God told him to live. He endorsed God's Law with his mind. He should live a holy life. He should exhibit a perfect standard of behavior.

But there is also what Paul calls the *"law in my members"* (v. 23). His bodily members took sides with the law of sin. His eyes looked with lust, his ears delighted in gossip. He was virtually torn apart by these conflicting laws. Moreover, he discovered that as a defeated saint he was doing exactly the same thing he had done as a doomed sinner. He was still trying in his own strength to produce the kind of life God expects.

Then he discovered the secret. "It is through Jesus Christ our Lord," he cried. It is trusting, not trying. The same Christ who gave him *eternal* life now offered him *victorious* life. "I thank God," was Paul's final sigh of blessed relief.

Devotion 58

THE GROANING OF THE COMFORTER

ROMANS 8:26-27

In his great treatise on the Christian life in Romans 8, Paul tells us of the groaning of the *Comforter*, of the groaning of the *creation*, and of the groaning of the *Christian*. In verses 26–27, it is the Holy Spirit he has in mind, the one the Lord Jesus called "the Comforter." Think of it! The third person of the Godhead is *groaning*. But that is what sin does. Hosea reminds us that sin not only breaks God's laws but it also breaks God's heart.

The word for "groanings" is *stenagmos*. It is used to describe the groanings of the Hebrew slaves in Egypt (Acts 7:34). The word is used in Romans 8 to describe the groaning of the Holy Spirit. It points to an inward, unexpressed feeling. Significantly, the word is in the plural here, intensifying the anguish.

Paul first sets before us *revealed truth about prayer*. He reminds us of two things. He shows us *how helpless we are*: "We know not what we should pray for as we ought." And he shows us *how helpful He is*: "Likewise the Spirit also helpeth our infirmities." Most church prayer meetings reveal how inadequate many of our prayers are. Prayer requests seem to consist of a long roll call of the sick, the sad, and the suffering. The Lord's prayers and Paul's prayers are occupied mostly with spiritual rather than physical or material things.

The Holy Spirit "helpeth," Paul says. The word is used in Luke 10:40 by Martha when she needed some down-to-earth help in the kitchen. Annoyed that she was tied to the kitchen while her sister Mary sat in the shade talking with Jesus and His disciples, Martha said to the Lord, "Bid her therefore that she *help* me." It is no accident, surely, that the very name "Comforter" is "*Paraclete*," meaning one "called alongside to help."

We have here, too, not only revealed truth about prayer, but also *real travail in prayer.* "The Spirit . . . maketh intercession for us with groanings which cannot be uttered" (Rom. 8:26). J. B. Phillips paraphrases, "His Spirit within us is actually praying for us in those agonizing longings which cannot be uttered."[1]

But there is more! We have here *remarkable triumph in prayer.* Romans continues, "He that searcheth the hearts knoweth what is in the mind of the Spirit, because he maketh intercession for the saints according to the will of God."

In other words, the Holy Spirit *knows my heart.* "He searcheth the hearts." He can read us like a book. He knows us better than we know ourselves. Then, too, He *knows His own mind.* He "knoweth what is the mind of the Spirit." He has already made up His mind about every situation in which we find ourselves, and He never makes mistakes. Finally, He *knows God's will*—"He maketh intercession for the saints according to the will of God." Therefore, it is absolutely impossible for the Holy Spirit ever to ask for a wrong thing or ever to get a "no" answer. How wonderful that He is on our side, and by our side, at all times.

---

1. J. B. Phillips, *The New Testament in Modern English* (New York: Macmillan, 1958).

Devotion 59

FOREKNOWN

ROMANS 8:29-30

The passage moves us steadily forward from a dateless, timeless past to an endless, eternal prospect in ages yet unborn but yet to be— *Foreknown! Predestinated! Called! Justified! Glorified!* Mark the onward march of the words—five movements in a monumental process all initiated by God. First, we are brought *into the sphere of his wisdom—Foreknown!* It goes without saying that since God is omniscient, since He knows everything, He knows the future as well as the past. Our knowledge is *after*-knowledge. We know things *after* they have happened. God's knowledge is fore-knowledge. God can know things *before* they happen. Both kinds of knowledge depend on the fact that certain things happen. It is a matter of perspective.

As we live our lives, we establish all kinds of facts about ourselves. They are written indelibly into our personal history—the date of our birth, our circumstances, our decisions, the date of our conversion, the date of our death. All these, and a myriad of others besides, are facts we establish as we live our lives. After-knowledge (our kind of knowledge) sees these facts and writes them down as *history*. God sees the same facts and writes them down also as *prophecy*. So, we are foreknown. God brings us into the sphere of His wisdom.

Second, we are brought *under the sovereignty of his will.* We are *predestinated!* Based upon His foreknowledge of our acceptance of Christ, God determined certain things for us, all those things that accompany salvation. Specifically, Paul tells us that God predetermines that every child of His will one day be like Jesus. In fact, so strong is this determination in God's mind that it is already done. We are going to be conformed to the image of His Son. God has sovereignly decreed it. We are predestinated to that end. Nothing can prevent it. All things will work together to ensure it. The word that declares it is in the past tense. So far as God is concerned, it is already done.

Third, we are brought *under the sound of His Word.* We are *called!* God's call is universal. Paul reminded the people of Athens that God "commandeth *all men every where* to repent" (Acts 17:30). God does not close the Bible until three times in one short verse He issues a universal call—"Come! Come! Come!" (Rev. 22:17). But that call becomes effective only when we respond. When Adam and Eve sinned, God called. In time, both responded. Adam declared his faith at once. He called his wife Eve, "the mother of all living" (Gen. 3:20). Eve declared her faith at a later date. She called her firstborn Cain, and confessed her belief in the promise of God, saying literally, "I have gotten the Man, even Jehovah." So God calls, and people respond.

Fourth, we are brought *under the shadow of His will.* We are *justified!* Justification is a much better thing than mere forgiveness. In order to be forgiven, a person has to plead guilty. You cannot pardon an innocent person. To be justified means that you are so declared righteous by God that the Law, even God Himself, can find no ground for impeachment. When we are saved, God can find no ground for impeachment. When we are saved, God puts us "in Christ." When He looks at us, He sees Him and all His righteousness. So He declares us to be righteous, justified!

Fifth, we are brought *into the splendor of His world.* We are *glorified!* This, also, is in the past tense. It is in the future, so far as we are concerned; but it is already done, so far as God is concerned. "Eye hath not seen," says Paul, "nor ear heard, . . . the things which God hath prepared for them that love him" (1 Cor. 2:9). There lies ahead for us what Paul calls an "exceeding and eternal weight of glory" (2 Cor. 4:17). Blessed be God our God!

Devotion 60

NO FOE! NO FEAR!

ROMANS 8:35–39

In concluding his treatise on the eternal security of the believer, Paul tells us two things. First, he tells us that *no foe can daunt us* (vv. 35–37).

Think of the long list of Paul's sufferings, which he gives in 2 Corinthians 11: prison sentences, beatings, stonings, shipwrecks. The list goes on and on. "In all these things," he was, "more than conqueror."

Or look at Peter, imprisoned by Herod, sentenced to death, scheduled to be executed on the morrow. What is he doing? Bemoaning his fate? No! Is he facing his cell, summoning his resolve, vowing to die like a man? *No!* He is *asleep!* He is not only conqueror; he is *more* than conqueror. No foe can daunt him, not even the monstrous Herod who ruled his little world.

Then, too, Paul tells us that *no fear can haunt us* (vv. 38–39). Paul parades a host of possibilities for our inspection, all of them potential disturbers of our peace.

There is *the inevitable*. Death awaits us all. It is the king of terrors. It separates friend from friend, husband from wife, mother from child. Can death separate us from the love of God? Of course not! Jesus has conquered death and all its powers. He says, "I am alive for evermore . . . and have the keys of hell and of death" (Rev. 1:18).

There is *the invisible*. Can invisible angels disturb our peace? Can principalities and powers separate us from God's love? No! Among the ranks of the angels, there are thrones and dominions (angelic beings loyal to God), and there are "principalities and powers" (angelic beings loyal to Satan). There are the rulers of this world's darkness, and there are wicked spirits in high places. All have been utterly shattered and defeated by Christ at Calvary and are now chained to the chariot wheels of His triumph (Col. 2:15).

There is *the inescapable*. "Can *things present* separate us from God's love?" Obviously they cannot because Jesus is ever present. He says, "Lo, I am with you always, even unto the end of the world" (Matt. 28:20). To get at us, those things that might haunt us have to get past Him. As for *things to come*, He is the coming One and is so portrayed from Genesis to Revelation. Well might we sing:

> 'Midst the darkness, storm, and sorrow
> One bright gleam I see;
> Well I know the blessed morrow
> Christ will come for me.[1]

Moreover, "in the ages to come" God intends to show us "the exceeding riches of his grace in his kindness toward us through Christ Jesus" (Eph. 2:7).

There is the *incalculable*—can height or depth haunt us or harm us? No indeed! Christ is not only at home in the heights, but He also has put them beneath our feet. We are already seated with Him in heavenly places (Eph. 1:3, 21). As for the depths, He has been down to the bottom, down to "the lower parts of the earth" (Eph. 4:9–10) and has been down there as Conqueror, as the mighty victor over sin and death and hell. There is nothing for us to fear down there. He has made sure of that.

Finally, there is the *inconceivable*. What about "any other creature"? There is no creature on earth, no creature in the highest heavens, or in the deepest depths, no creature unknown or unimagined, that can harm us. He has created all things, and all creatures bend at last before His will and own Him to be their Lord. Creatures unknown may have vast power, but He has omnipotent power.

Nothing can separate us from the love of *Christ Jesus our Lord*. That phrase is Paul's closing word in four successive chapters in Romans, chapters 5–8. In chapter 5 Jesus Christ our Lord *separates*. In chapter 6 Jesus Christ our Lord *saves*. In chapter 7 Jesus Christ our Lord *sanctifies*, and in chapter 8 Jesus Christ our Lord *secures*. Hallelujah! What a Savior!

---

1.   Gerhardt Ter Steegen, "The Bride," in *Hymns of Ter Steegen, Suso, and Others*, trans. Frances Bevan (London: Nisbet, 1904).

Devotion 61

ALL ARE YOURS

Some years ago the wife of a friend of mine lay dying from a particularly painful kind of cancer. My friend loved his wife dearly. The thought of her dying wracked his very soul. The sight of her dying in agony drove him to distraction.

Then the emissaries of a religious group assured him that if he had enough faith, his wife would be healed. When I went to see him, he was pacing the corridors of the hospital, convinced that his lack of faith was the reason she was still slowly, painfully dying in her bed. This cruel "teaching" had just about finished him. I took him down to the coffee shop and sought to comfort him. I turned in my Bible to 1 Corinthians 3:21–23.

"Now, Claude," I said, "look at some of the things the Holy Spirit says are yours—Paul, Apollos, the world, life, death, things present, things to come. These things are yours, given to you by a Sovereign God, one who controls all the factors of time, matter, and space.

"*No matter who*—'whether Paul, or Apollos, or Cephas.' These men represent true apostles and true Bible teachers. We are to listen to such as these, giving honor where honor is due, avoiding false apostles and false prophets. We listen to those truly called, gifted, and anointed by God, thankful for any measure of truth they have to impart.

"*No matter where*—'the world.' It makes no difference to the Lord whether we are in this town or that one, this hospital or some other. He rules the world.

"*No matter what*—'life, or death.' Jesus is the life. He has conquered death and holds its key.

"*No matter when*—'things present, or things to come.' Jesus transcends all time. He has conquered time. He inhabits eternity. The past, the present, and the future are all the same to Him.

"Now notice," I said, "that God has *given* all these things to you. All of them, in their own proper time and place, are yours. Right now one of these is especially yours—*death!* God has given death to you as His gift. That may sound strange, but think what it means.

"Mary is going to die because her condition is terminal. The thought troubles you; it torments you. But it is so. She is going to die. You must not blame yourself and torture yourself on that account. Her death is not your fault. No, indeed! God is now *giving* you death as His kind and living gift. He is too loving to be unkind. He is too wise to make any mistakes. He is too powerful to be hindered. Death is about releasing your beloved from her suffering and pain. It is soon to open for her the gates of glory. It will lift her into that land where they count not time by years, to where Christ sits at the right hand of God. She will be absent from that pain-wracked body of hers, and she will be present with the Lord. All this, death will do for her and you. She will cease to suffer. She will be at rest, safe in the arms of Jesus. And you will be able to rest in the certain knowledge that she is with the Lord. Then *time* ('things to come'), another of God's gifts to you, will heal your hurts as well."

The lines of anguish slowly faded from his face. "Thank you," he said, "I needed that."

Devotion 62

WHAT MANNER OF LOVE

1 CORINTHIANS 13; 1 JOHN 3:1-3

God's love is *love that is sovereignly bestowed*. We are invited to consider "what *manner* of love" it is that God bestows upon us (1 John 3:1). "God is love," we read (1 John 4:8). "God is light," we also read (1 John 1:5). The one divine attribute illustrates the other. Pass light through a prism, and it breaks up into seven colors. Pass sunlight through the storm, and it will produce a rainbow. Take the seven colors of the spectrum, and put them into motion; and they will merge into one—the color of light.

Just as there are seven colors that compose light, so there are nine elements that compose love. Paul describes them in 1 Corinthians 13. They are—patience, kindness, generosity, humility, courtesy, unselfishness, good temper, guilelessness, and sincerity.

Take the nine components of love, and put them into motion; and they all merge into the essence of what God is: *love*. God proposes to bestow His love, in all its completeness and according to its various components, on us. *That* is "the manner of love" God sovereignly bestows. It expresses itself uniquely thus: "That we should be called the sons of God" (1 John 3:1). We who were sinners of Adam's ruined race are now *children of God*. The hymn writer puts it like this:

> Great God of wonders! All Thy ways
> Are matchless, Godlike and divine;
> But the fair glories of Thy grace
> More Godlike and unrivaled shine.[1]

God is omnipotent, of course! God is omniscient; it goes without saying! God is omnipresent; that is so. But here is the supreme wonder:

---

1. Samuel Davies, "Great God of Wonders."

God is love. That is not just an attribute, however. It is the ultimate face of His being. He bestows this love sovereignly on us, calling us *sons* of God.

God's love also is *love that is sweetly confirmed.* "Beloved, now are we the sons of God" (1 John 3:2). Blessed be God our God! That means that we, too, are to shed love abroad in this dark world of sin.

Henry Drummond once said, "In the heart of Africa, among the great lakes, I have come across black men and women who remembered the only white man they ever saw before—David Livingstone. And as you cross his footsteps in that dark continent, men's faces light up as they speak of the kind doctor who passed there years ago."[2] "Beloved, now are we the sons of God."

Finally, the love of God is *love that is suddenly complete.* "It doth not yet appear what we shall be: but we know that, when he shall appear, we shall be like him; for we shall see him as he is" (1 John 3:2). Theologians talk about perfect sanctification and progressive sanctification. The moment we are saved we are made perfect in Christ. "For he hath made him to be sin for us, who knew no sin; that we might be made the righteousness of God in him" (2 Cor. 5:21). God sees us robed in the righteousness of Christ. We are as fit for heaven as though we were already there. We have perfect sanctification. God looks at us in Christ and sees Him. That is perfect sanctification.

However, we are still in the body and have to do daily battle with the flesh. Our standing is perfect; our state is not. The indwelling Holy Spirit works with our human spirit to produce the fruit of the Spirit. We are to be progressively "fruitful in every good work, and increasing in the knowledge of God" (Col. 1:10).

But one of these days He Himself will appear. We shall see Him as He is. Instantly we shall be like Him. That perfect sanctification, which now is only reckoned to us (Rom. 6:7, 11–13), will be realized by us.

The old chorus only expresses our longing:

> Be like Jesus, this my song,
> In the home and in the throng;

---

2. Henry Drummond, *The Greatest Thing in the World,* 1880.

Be like Jesus, all day long!
I would be like Jesus.[3]

When we see Him as He is, the transformation will take place. We shall be like Jesus indeed.

---

3.   James Rowe, "I Would Be Like Jesus," 1911.

Devotion 63

THE GRACE OF OUR LORD JESUS CHRIST

2 CORINTHIANS 8:9

Paul takes it for granted that we know at least something of the grace of the Lord Jesus Christ. Just the same, he challenges us to know more. He sets before us two things—two things calculated to stir us to the depth of our being. First, he gives us a glimpse of *superlative grace*: "Ye know the grace of our Lord Jesus Christ, that, though he was rich, yet for your sakes he became poor."

We know that He was rich, but we have no idea how rich He really was. We sometimes sing:

> My Father is rich in houses and lands,
> He holdeth the wealth of the world in His hands![1]

But that is only a small part of it. In the land from whence He came, they pave their streets with gold. The towering walls of His great city are made of jasper, its gates of solid pearl, and its twelve foundations are ablaze with priceless gems. Before He came down here, He sat in splendor on a great white throne while shining seraphim hung upon His words and rushed to do His will. All His ministers were a flame of fire. All the vast galactic empires of the stars belonged to Him. Had He so desired He could have created galaxies of gold.

So then, we know that He was rich, but we cannot tell how rich He was. Only one or two of Adam's race have ever been to His land and returned to tell the tale. Even then they had difficulty telling what they saw. Paul was there and declared that what he saw was untranslatable. John was there, and he resorts to symbolic language when telling us

---

I.   Harriet E. Buell, "A Child of the King," 1877.

what that place is like. So, then, we know that He was rich. We do not know how rich He was.

We know, too, that for our sakes, He became poor. But, again, we do not know how poor He was. He was born in a borrowed barn. When He wanted to teach the crowding multitudes, He had to borrow Simon Peter's boat to be His stage. To feed the hungry multitudes, He had to borrow a little lad's lunch. To ride through Jerusalem in triumph in fulfillment of an ancient prophecy, He had to borrow a donkey from a friend. To keep His last Passover, He had to borrow someone's upper room. He died upon another man's cross and was buried in a borrowed tomb. Foxes had their holes, and birds of the air had their nests, but He had nowhere to lay His head.

Then, too, we have *superlative gain.* "Why," we ask, "did He who was so superlatively rich become so startlingly poor?" "That ye," says Paul, "through his poverty might be rich." First, He canceled all our debt. We are the ten-thousand-talent debtors of whom Jesus spoke. We are those who are bankrupt with nothing to pay. He took all our debt, ours and ten thousand times ten thousand other debts beside. He took it to Calvary and beggared Himself in order to cancel it all.

But there is more! He has made us rich. He has made us children of God and joint-heirs with Himself. He has seated us with Himself in the heavenlies in a realm beyond the sky, and He has endowed us with all the riches of His grace. Now He is building for us mansions in glory, and He has promised us that where He is, there we shall be also.

Such is the grace of our Lord Jesus Christ. "Selah!" as David would say, "What do you think of that?"

Devotion 64

DOCTOR LUKE

COLOSSIANS 4:14; PHILEMON 24; 2 TIMOTHY 4:11

L uke is mentioned only three times in the New Testament. He was a Greek. Possibly he was the "man of Macedonia" who appeared to the missionary in a vision and turned Paul's steps toward Europe (Acts 16:9–10).

We recognize him as *a very brilliant man.* We are indebted to him for what he tells us about *the Christ.* Luke's gospel has been called "the most beautiful book in the world." It was probably written during the period of Paul's imprisonment at Caesarea, or possibly during Paul's imprisonment at Rome. Luke had access to many of the people concerned, and he had a thorough knowledge of the facts. Doubtless he would often confer with Paul about various facts he was investigating. His gospel is rich in stories of human interest. He records seven miracles and nineteen parables mentioned nowhere else, including the parables of the good Samaritan, the prodigal son, and the rich fool. Such Pauline words as faith, repentance, mercy, and forgiveness show up often.

Then, too, we are indebted to Luke for what he tells us about *the church.* The book of Acts, written by Luke, forms an essential bridge between the Gospels and the Epistles. With consummate skill, and from a thorough acquaintance with the facts, Luke traces the early history of the church from an upper room in Jerusalem to a prison house in Rome. He weaves his story around the personalities of Simon, Stephen, and Saul. He points out the founding emphasis, the forward emphasis, and the foreign emphasis of the church and leaves the story dangling, incomplete, and unfinished. Countless other chapters, covering some two thousand years of time, would yet need to be written; but that was far beyond the scope of even Luke's busy pen.

Then, too, Luke was *a very beloved man.* He was one of Paul's dearest and closest friends. Paul was not a well man. When we think of the beatings, the scourgings, the shipwrecks, the imprisonments, and the dangers he had endured, it is little wonder he needed the constant attendance of a physician. When Paul finally arrived back in Philippi, where Luke lived, after having gone through some of the horrendous experiences he describes in 2 Corinthians 11, Luke doubtless insisted on giving his friend a thorough overhaul. "That does it, Paul," we can hear him say. "From now on, I'm traveling with you." Paul calls him the "beloved physician" (Col. 4:14).

Finally, he was *a very brave man.* When Paul appealed to Caesar around A.D. 59, to escape the peril he was in at the hands of the Jewish and Roman authorities, Nero had not yet shown his true colors. But times changed for the worse. In A.D. 64 Nero set fire to Rome and blamed the Christians, and a nightmare persecution broke out. Paul was remanded back to prison, not this time to his own hired house and the privileges secured by his Roman citizenship, but to the so-called Steps of Groaning and into the dreaded Mammertime Prison. There he was stripped and lowered into the terrible lower dungeon, the infamous Tullianum. There he would await death. Some of his colleagues he sent away. Some, like Demas, abandoned him. Only his beloved Doctor Luke remained.

One morning the executioners came for Paul. Doubtless the daring doctor accompanied him to the place of death. At this point Luke disappears. But we shall hear more about this brave man one of these days, at the judgment seat of Christ, when the full tale will be told; and Jesus will be heard to say: "Well done, Luke! Well done."

Devotion 65

THE LORD SHALL DESCEND FROM HEAVEN

1 THESSALONIANS 4:13–18

The shout will shatter the age-long silence of the Godhead. It is a silence that began with the triumphant shout of the dying Christ on the cross at Calvary. It has lasted already for nearly two thousand years. It has been silence long, prolonged, and absolute, a silence that has caused scoffers to blaspheme and saints to stumble. But what other answer could God give to the crime of Calvary? It was either silence or wrath. God chose silence. But the silence will be broken one of these days. The church will be taken up with a shout, and wrath will come down with a roar. It will be rapture for the church and wrath for the world.

First, there are *the sounds*. It will all begin with "a shout": "the Lord himself shall descend from heaven with a shout," Paul says (1 Thess. 4:16). Only three times in the Bible does Jesus shout. He shouted at the tomb of Lazarus, and a dead man came to life (John 11:43–44). He shouted on the cross, and many bodies of the saints which slept, arose and came out of their graves after His resurrection and went into the Holy City and appeared unto many (Matt. 27:50, 52–53). He will shout at the time of His coming again, and a whole church will rise—a multitude that no one can number. The shout is for the church.

It will be accompanied by "the voice of the archangel" (1 Thess. 4:16). The voice of the archangel is for the angels, to summon the angels for war. The rapture of the church will mean that the amnesty is over. The nationals of heaven are taken home, and God will declare war on a world that murdered His Son. The angels come into their own. They appear in chapter after chapter of the Apocalypse.

Then, too, there will be "the trump of God" (v. 16). The trump of

God is for Israel. The fact that the nation of Israel has been reborn and is back in the land tells us that end-time events are upon us. The time of Jacob's trouble cannot be too far off. These are the sounds—the shout, the voice, and the trump.

Then there are *the sights*. There are two of them. The first is *the resurrection* of all those who have died in Christ. "The dead in Christ shall rise first," Paul says, those whose names are written in the Lamb's book of life. They hoped against hope that the Lord would come in their lifetime, but death came instead. However, they will rise. The resurrection of Christ is the guarantee of that. They will come bounding from their tombs shouting, "O grave, where is thy victory?" (I Cor. 15:55).

Then comes *the rapture* of all those who are alive and remain when Jesus comes for His church. They will leap into the sky, changed, transformed in a moment, in the twinkling of an eye. As they soar upward to the courts of bliss, they will cry: "O death, where is thy sting?" And one and all, the living saints and those who once were dead, will become just like Jesus, and their bodies will be just like His.

And then there will be *the songs*. There will be a song of *comfort in the gloom*: "Comfort one another with these words," Paul says (I Thess. 4:18). The Christians at Thessalonica had lost some of their number to death, and they thought they had lost them forever. Paul's letter was intended to comfort them, as well as believers in all the ages yet to come. The philosophers, scientists, and cultists of the world have no comfort to offer when death moves in. Only the gospel offers us the blessed hope of the coming again of One who has the keys of death and of hell (Rev. 1:18).

And, finally, there will be the song of *consummation in the glory*. With the Lord! With the Lord! What more could we want than that?

> He and I, in that bright glory,
> One deep joy shall share—
> Mine, to be for ever with Him;
> His, that I am there.[1]

I.   Gerhardt Ter Steegen, "The Bride," in *Hymns of Ter Steegen, Suso, and Others*, trans. Frances Bevan (London: Nisbet, 1904).

THE MAN OF SIN

2 THESSALONIANS 2:3-12

It seems there had been some kind of spirit utterance in the infant church at Thessalonica. Someone had spoken with a lying "tongue." Apparently, there also had been a "voice of prophecy," but it had not been the Holy Spirit's voice. Like the infant church's gift of "tongues," its gift of prophecy also could be imitated by a lying spirit. The Thessalonians were far too ready to take such manifestations as of God without testing the spirits to make sure that the communication had come from God.

In those days, before the completion of the New Testament canon of Scripture, tongues and prophecy were still valid gifts. If caution was necessary in those days, how much more skeptical we should be in these days when these foundational gifts have been withdrawn (I Cor. 13:8; I John 4:1–3).

That was not all. There also had been a forged letter purporting to have come from Paul. Thus the deception was threefold (a lying tongue, a false prophecy, and a forged letter), and a threefold cord is not easily broken. The Bereans would not have been so gullible. We read that they were "more noble than those in Thessalonica, in that they received the word with all readiness of mind, and searched the scriptures daily, whether those things were so" (Acts 17:11).

Paul took advantage of this deception in the Thessalonian church to unveil a larger deception—Satan's most secret plans for the end times. We have, first, *the unveiling of Satan's man*: "Let no man deceive you by any means," says Paul (2 Thess. 2:3), using a double negative to reinforce the warning. He tells us that before the Man of Sin can be revealed, there has to be "a falling away first," and overwhelming apostasy. Satan's man is called "the man of sin" and also "the son of perdition." We generally recognize this prodigy of wickedness as the Antichrist. He is called "the beast" in the Apocalypse. He is "the little horn" of Daniel 7, the final

Gentile world ruler. He is supported by an apostate Jew, called "the false prophet" (Rev. 19:20). The Antichrist will be killed but will come back to life again (17:8). In his early career, he is called the beast "out of the sea" (13:1) but, in his later career, he is the beast out of the Abyss (17:8–14).

Paul tells the Thessalonians that the Holy Spirit, working through the church, is at work in the world today, holding back the rising tides of wickedness. In the end, however, the godless forces working in society will produce the Man of Sin, once the Holy Spirit removes the restraint. The rapture of the church will make it possible for Satan to bring in his man. "*Then* shall that Wicked [one] be revealed," Paul says (2 Thess. 2:8).

Immediately after the rapture, there will not only be a sudden acceleration in every kind of wickedness; but chaos will descend upon the world (Rev. 6). The Devil will then produce his man. He will revive the old Roman Empire, sweep away all opposition, and take control of the whole world. "Who is able to make war with him?" (Rev. 13:4), the hesitant nations will say, as they sign up as members of the new global empire.

Once global power is in his hands, the Antichrist will force people to receive his mark and worship his image. He will then launch a global persecution of the Jews and all who hold the Judeo-Christian ethic. In the end, God's judgments will weaken the Antichrist. The nations of the East will rebel and mobilize against him and will march westward, setting the stage for Armageddon and the return of Christ to reign.

Paul warns the Thessalonians against unbelief. Unbelievers left behind at the rapture of the church, people who have heard the gospel and rejected it, will believe the Devil's lies. Indeed, God Himself will withdraw Himself from all those who choose the lie over His Son, who is the Truth (John 14:6). It is always that way. People who disbelieve or ignore the truth lay themselves open to believe a lie. It is always so. Let the unbeliever beware.

Devotion 67

PHILEMON AND ONESIMUS

PHILEMON 1:1–25

Colossae was a small, sleepy market town on the Lycus River, a hundred miles from Ephesus. It was once a busy enough place on the main east-west road, but time had passed it by. It is famous now only because Paul wrote a letter to the church in town. Philemon, a wealthy citizen of Colossae, had become a Christian through the ministry of Paul. Perhaps he had met Paul at Ephesus. We do not know. But Philemon, his wife, and his son were leading members of the Colossian church.

Onesimus was Philemon's slave. Doubtless Philemon was a good enough master, but Onesimus coveted his freedom. The lot of a slave, at best, was to be subject to the whim of his owner. He could be scourged or sold or slaughtered. He had no rights. He was just a piece of property. The name "Onesimus" means "profitable," but he certainly was not profitable to Philemon. He robbed Philemon and then ran for refuge to Rome. There he could hide from the one to whom he belonged. He is a type and picture of all of us, runaways from God.

The slums of Rome, Onesimus thought, would be a perfect hiding place; but he reckoned without God. Somehow he ran into Paul who, though a prisoner, had considerable liberty and his own hired house.

"Ah! Onesimus! What are you doing here?" we can almost hear Paul say. The long and the short of it was that Paul led Onesimus to Christ. "And now, my friend," he said, "we'll have to send you back." The least Onesimus could expect was to be scourged. Custom and the law would all be on the slave owner's side, and other slave owners would expect Philemon to be severe. Leniency to a runaway slave was rare. Onesimus was alarmed. "I'll be your mediator," said Paul. "You don't belong to me. You belong to another. Back you must go, no matter what." It was no cheap gospel that was preached in those days.

So Onesimus went back to Philemon, but he was not expected to plead his own case. Paul gave him a memo to be given to his master. Perhaps he read it to him: "Onesimus," he wrote, "is my child . . . my very heart. If you count me as a partner, receive him as you receive me." Paul did not ask that Onesimus be received back as a slave, but as though he were Paul himself. How would Philemon have received Paul? Would he have put him back there in the slave compound? Never! He would have killed for him the fatted calf, placed him in the seat of honor at his table, put him in the guest room, and crowned him with glory and honor.

Philemon might well have balked. Onesimus had stolen money from him. "Put that to my account," said Paul. "As for the future good behavior of your returned slave, well, all I can say is that from now on, if it's a *slave* you want, you'll find him up to his name, profitable indeed."

But there was more to it than that. Onesimus was now "a brother beloved." Calvary abolishes all class distinction between believers. It puts master and servant on the same footing.

So Onesimus said good-bye to Paul and, clutching this memo tightly in his hand, he headed back to the one to whom he belonged. The story is a perfect little gem. The only thing that stood between him and a cross was a mediator back there in Rome and a memorandum of less than a hundred forty words.

We do not know how Onesimus was received. Paul, however, had no doubts. In the epistle he wrote to the Colossians about this time or soon after, he mentions Onesimus. He refers to him as "a faithful and beloved brother, who is one of you" (Col. 4:9). And can we doubt it? Though Paul organized no marches or demonstrations, this memo of his struck a blow against slavery and for freedom unsurpassed.

Devotion 68

A PERFECT HIGH PRIEST

HEBREWS 7:26

There are three things about our High Priest that enables Him to meet all our needs. First, *He is holy*. Picture the camp of Israel. The wilderness wanderings have brought the people to the frontiers of Moab. Down from the hills comes a Moabite, a man under a curse (Deut. 23:3). He has seen the Hebrew tribes spread out before him in perfect order. He has seen the fiery, cloudy pillar overshadowing the camp. He may even have heard of the eloquent prophecies of Balaam regarding Moab and Israel (Num. 22–24; 31:16). He is filled with curiosity. He approaches the door of the tabernacle, and there he is stopped. But he is full of questions.

The man at the gate explains to the Moabite that of all days for him to come, he happens to have come on the Day of Atonement. The high priest, yonder in the gorgeous robes, will soon enter into the Holy of Holies itself. He will take the blood of a goat with him to sprinkle on the mercy seat.

The man from Moab asks a question: "And what about that bullock over there?" He is told: "The goat is to atone for the sins of everyone, but the bullock is for the sins of the high priest! Before he can confess the sins of the people, he must first confess his own. Indeed, his sins are much worse in the sight of God than anyone else's. That's why he needs a bullock, while a goat will do for everyone else."

There is something disappointing about that. We want a priest who is holy. The nation of Israel in some fifteen hundred years never had such a high priest. But that is exactly what we have in Jesus—a holy High Priest.

Then, too, our high priest has something else we need in a priest. *He is human*. As the conversation between the Moabite and the man at the gate continues, someone barges in. "Of course, we need a holy priest," he says, "but there is something very cold, to my mind, about goodness in the abstract. I find the thought of an absolutely sinless high priest formidable. I want someone a little more human—someone who knows from experience what it is like to be full of infirmities. I don't want a sinful high priest, but I certainly want a sympathetic one—someone who knows what it is like to be tempted and tried." Thank God for Jesus! He is thoroughly human. He understands us wonderfully well.

Finally, *He is helpful*. Someone else speaks up, adding to the conversation: "I want someone who can be helpful. Why, even the high priest of Israel can only stay in the Holy of Holies long enough to sprinkle the blood. He certainly cannot remain in there. He cannot go in there whenever he likes. And, in any case, this tabernacle is only a temporary affair. None of this is very helpful to me.

"I want someone *bigger* than Moses, someone *better* than Aaron, and someone *beyond* even Melchizedek. I want someone who is human but is more than human. I want someone who is sinless but also sympathetic—someone who not only knows me but also loves me. I want someone who can deal with my sins and can enter the Holy of Holies in heaven on my behalf. I need someone who can invite me to enter into the Holy of Holies. I need someone who can satisfy God, and silence Satan, and still my conscience, and make me good."

Well, thank God, we have such a high priest. His name is Jesus. God says, "For such an high priest became us, who is holy, harmless, undefiled, separate from sinners, and made higher than the heavens" (Heb. 7:26). Thank God for Him.

Devotion 69

LO, I COME

HEBREWS 10:7-9

L o, I come (in the volume of the book it is written of me,) to do thy will, O God." The context shows that from the beginning two things would be needed to rescue fallen humans—a book and a body. Both are mentioned here.

First, there is the *Book*. It took some four thousand years to write that Book. It involved people drawn from various walks of life. It is a book of *startling prophecies*, many of them focused on the two comings of Christ. It is a book of *symbolic pictures*, pictures we call "types." These are coded prophecies of things to come. Consider just one, the slaying of the Passover lamb.

The lamb had to be taken on the tenth day of the first month of the Jewish year. The Lord triumphantly entered Jerusalem on that very day—the tenth day of Nisan. The lamb had to be tethered on the day it was bought. On that day the Sanhedrin "bought" Jesus by paying Judas thirty pieces of silver to betray Him. The Lord stayed close to Jerusalem from then on, under the eyes of Judas. Each night He went out to nearby Bethany, and each day He came back to Jerusalem. That was the length of His tether. Like the Old Testament paschal lamb, He was kept under constant observation.

The Passover lamb was killed on the fourteenth day of the first month—the very day of the crucifixion—"the preparation of the Passover," the day was called. The lamb was killed "in the evening" (Exod. 12:6), or, literally, "between the two evenings." Josephus identifies this as being between the sixth hour (noon) and the ninth hour (3:00 PM). That was when the Jews killed their lambs. And that was when they killed Jesus, the true Paschal Lamb. So, to the year, to the month, to the day, to the hour, God's Lamb was slain—such is the accuracy of the Book.

This brings us to *the body*. "Sacrifice and offering thou wouldest not, but a body hast thou prepared me" (Heb. 10:5). These are the very words Jesus spoke as recorded by the Spirit of God. The body was necessary so that God the Son could become the Son of Man. It was necessary, too, so that He could be offered as a sacrifice, once and for all.

It was "prepared," the Holy Spirit says. The Greek word is *katartizo*. It means "to mend." It is used of James and John mending their nets. The human body, damaged by the fall and subject to disease, deformity, and death, was "mended" for Jesus. His was a perfect body, one completely undamaged by sin. It was free from congenital weakness and from latent weakness. He was free from sin, free from sickness, free from accidents, and free from all bodily harm—"a lamb without blemish and without spot" (1 Peter 1:19).

It was the Holy Spirit who went to work in the womb of the woman to create that body. He guided the creation of the trillions of cells that made up that holy body. Finally, when it was finished, Jesus was born, and the angels came down in droves to gaze upon the marvel of it all.

Jesus lived in that body, on this planet in space, for thirty-three and a half years. Then He gave that body to be broken. We see that body bowed to the earth and shaken with sobs in Gethsemane. We see it bruised and buffeted at Gabbatha and scourged to the bone in Pilate's hall. We see it crowned with thorns, smitten, and spat upon. We see it, arms outstretched to save, spiked to a cross at Golgotha. Finally, we see it in its grave, sealed and secured. It slept in total incorruption. And on the third day it burst forth from the tomb. Now it is enthroned on high.

So a Book has been written. A body has been risen. And now we have a Savior, Christ the Lord! Blessed be God our God.

Devotion 70

INTO THE HOLIEST

HEBREWS 10:19–20

The veil of the temple was a gorgeous curtain woven of the finest linen, dyed scarlet, blue, and purple, as thick as a person's hand, and embroidered with the forbidding figures of the cherubim. Its sole purpose was to provide a barrier between God and human beings. We notice that our text answers four questions—What? Where? Why? and Who? "Boldness to enter"—that's *what*. "Into the holiest"—that's *where*. "By the blood of Jesus"—that's *why*. "Through the veil, that is to say, his flesh"—that's *who*.

What? We have "boldness to enter." And what boldness it is! No Jew would think of entering there. King Uzziah became a leper for trying to enter there. But in this age, we have boldness to enter where prophets, priests, and kings all feared to tread. The entire protocol of the Old Testament has been changed. Now we are invited in where, for Israel, the veil barred the way.

The story is told of a small boy who stood at the gate of Buckingham Palace, hoping to catch a glimpse of the king. A well-dressed man drove up and got out of his car. He glanced at the eager face of the boy. "Come with me," he said, extending his hand. The policeman stood aside, the gate was opened wide, and a soldier presented arms. Up flights of stairs they went, through sumptuous apartments, on to a private suite in the north wing, half a mile away from the kitchens. "This is my friend, Willy," said the man when at last they arrived in the presence of the king. "He wanted to see you. He took my hand, so I brought him on in. Sonny, this is the king. He's my father. I'm Edward, Prince of Wales."

That is what! We have taken hold of a hand, the nail-scarred hand, of the King's own Son. So we have boldness to enter, for He smoothes the way.

Where? "Into the holiest" we may enter. It was the innermost shrine of the temple, where a thrice-holy God sat enthroned and where holiness shone in the blinding light of the Shechinah. It was a holiness that could blaze out in judgment at any moment, as it did with Aaron's careless sons, Nadab and Abihu. These foolish men tried to approach God with their counterfeit fire. But Calvary has changed all that! We are now invited in, invited even to sit where the angel Gabriel dared only stand.

Why? The reason is simple. The blood of Jesus invites us in. The high priest of old could enter inside the veil once a year for a few fleeting moments, protected by the blood of a goat. We can come into the real Holy of Holies in heaven itself, protected by the blood of Jesus. That blood, shed at Calvary, is now present on the mercy seat in the Holy of Holies in heaven.

Who? We enter "by a new and living way, through the veil, that is to say, his flesh." That brings us back to Christ. "The Word was made flesh," John says, describing the incarnation of the Son of God. The flesh refers to His body, which houses both His sinless humanity and His awesome deity. As the veil was first hung and then rent, so was the body of Jesus. It was hung on the cross and rent with a spear. As He died on the tree, the veil was rent in the *temple*. A new and living way has been opened up for us into the immediate presence of a thrice-holy God! So let us boldly enter in.

Devotion 71

FAITH DENIED

HEBREWS 11:1

"F aith," says the Holy Spirit, "is the substance of things hoped for, the evidence of things not seen." The word for "substance" here is *hupostasis*. The same word is used to describe the person of the Lord Jesus as expressing the very image of God in human form (1:3). In everyday Greek the word was used to depict title deeds. A title deed gives substance to a person's claim to property. The word for "evidence" is *elenchos*. It means "proof."

Two thoughts emerge. Faith gives us the title deed to things hoped for, and it gives us all the evidence we need that certain things we have not yet seen are all they are said to be. In other words, faith has to do with things we *long for*, things still unsatisfied as yet; and it has to do with things we *look for*, things still unseen as yet. In both cases faith makes them substantial and real. Faith is not wishful thinking. "Faith cometh by hearing, and hearing by the word of God" (Rom. 10:17).

Abraham shows us how faith is the title deed, the guarantee, the substance, of things hoped for. Abraham longed for a son. The years passed, and the son did not come. He grew older. He passed the age when he could still hope.

Paul tells us that Abraham "against hope believed in hope. . . . And being not weak in faith, he considered not his own body now dead, when he was about an hundred years old, neither yet the deadness of Sarah's womb: He staggered not at the promise of God through unbelief; but was strong in faith, giving glory to God; And being fully persuaded that, what he had promised, he was able also to perform" (Rom. 4:18–21).

Abraham's faith in God was so strong that the thing he longed for was a real possession of his before ever the promised son was born. That is to say, he already had the boy's birth certificate in his hand (in God's pledged word), before he had the child in his arms. God's word was the ground of his faith and assurance. The thing he longed for was already his—by faith.

Noah shows us how faith is the evidence, the proof of things unseen. God told Noah He was going to send a flood. It seems likely that Noah had never seen a flood. Genesis 2:6 would indicate he had never even seen rain. He had never seen the windows of heaven opened or the fountains of the great deep erupt. Certainly he had never seen God act in universal, catastrophic judgment.

But God spoke, and Noah believed God and set out to obey Him by building the ark, even though there were no actual signs of the promised flood. In sure anticipation of things not seen as yet, but most surely to be expected in God's time, Noah built the ark. The threatened judgment was delayed for one hundred twenty years. The ark was finished at last. Still sure that the flood would come, Noah and his family entered the ark, and still the flood did not come. Nothing happened for a whole week, but Noah had no doubt. God's word was God's word. A week later the proof based on faith became proof based on fact. The rain began to fall.

The principle of faith, whether relating to things *longed for* or things *looked for*, applies to us as well. God's Word is sure.

THE WORSHIP OF CAIN

HEBREWS 11:4

By faith," we are told, "Abel offered unto God a more excellent sacrifice than Cain, by which he obtained witness that he was righteous." Thus, from the dawn of human history, two ways emerged—the broad way with its wide gate, its easy road, and its bitter end; and the narrow way with its one restricting gate, its hard road, and its glorious end. The one begins at the gate of the garden of God and runs by way of the cross to the city of God. The other begins at the gate of the garden of Cain and runs by way of the city of destruction to the caverns of the lost. Abel's way immediately produced a martyr. Cain's way simultaneously produced a murderer.

There are four characteristics of the worship of Cain. First, it substituted *reason for revelation*. Cain and Abel both had access to the same information. It had not taken their parents long to learn that human nakedness could not be covered with the fig leaves of human effort. Sin could be covered only by the shedding of blood. An innocent substitute had to die in their stead so that a fitting covering could be theirs. Thus redeemed, they stood before God, clothed at enormous cost.

Cain and Abel must have been told these things often. Hebrews 11 says it was by *faith* that Abel made his offering. Romans 10:17 reminds us that "faith cometh by hearing, and hearing by the word of God." So God must have made it clear and plain to both these boys that if He was to be approached at all, it must be by faith and it must be by blood. Such was the divine revelation.

Cain ignored the word of God. He substituted human reasoning for divine revelation. To his way of thinking, the way of the cross seemed monstrous. Right from the start, this liberal theologian set apart God's word and substituted his own carnal ideas.

Then, too, he substituted *trying for trusting*. Abel would speak words such as those we find in Augustus Toplady's old hymn, "Rock of Ages":

> Nothing in my hand I bring,
> Simply to Thy cross I cling;
> Naked, come to Thee for dress;
> Helpless, look to Thee for grace;
> Foul, I to the fountain fly;
> Wash me, Savior, or I die.[1]

"Nonsense!" said Cain. Salvation has to be earned. We have to work for it; we have to suffer and earn merit. This philosophy of Cain, of course, is the very essence of all false religion. Man-made religions call upon us to fast and pray and make pilgrimages and do penance and do good works. It is the way of Cain.

Moreover, Cain substituted *beauty for blood*. "Without shedding of blood," God declared, there is "no remission" of sin (Heb 9:22). "When I see the blood, I will pass over you," God said to Israel on the eve of their redemption (Exod. 12:13, 23). Cain would have none of it. He looked at Abel's altar, and he shuddered. His whole artistic soul rose up in revolt against such a "gospel of gore," as he (like modern liberal theologians) would possibly have described it. He had a better way, an aesthetically pleasing way. He planted a garden and toiled night and day. Then he built an altar of hewn stones and brought fragrant flowers and colorful fruits. He arranged them and rearranged them until he had obtained the desired effect. "Now that ought to please God," he said to his soul. It was beautiful! But it was all the fruit of the earth God had cursed and was useless as a means of salvation from sin.

Finally, he substituted *persecution for persuasion*. God rejected Cain's religion totally and absolutely, and Cain was furious. He went away in a rage. Then he went around and looked at Abel's altar, stained with blood, black with fire, reeking of death; and his blood boiled. Abel tried to reason with him, but a person committed to a false faith is the most unreasonable of people. Cain murdered Abel and then insolently said to God, "Am I my brother's keeper?" (Gen. 4:9). It was all a prelude to what the Bible calls "the way of Cain." But that is another story.

---

1.   Augustus Toplady, "Rock of Ages," 1776.

Devotion 73

HE LOOKED FOR A CITY

HEBREWS 11:8–10

By faith Abraham . . . obeyed." We begin with *the call*. Abraham was called "to go out into a place which he should after receive for an inheritance." Abraham was a native of the city of Ur, on the bank of the Euphrates. He seems to have been well-to-do. He was a descendant of Noah's son Shem, the one chosen by God to carry on the godly line. However, by the time Shem's descendants ran through eight or nine generations, the knowledge among them of the true and living God was just about lost. In all likelihood, Abraham was virtually a pagan, a worshiper of the moon—until the Holy Spirit began to work in his soul.

The time came when God revealed Himself to Abraham. He gave him his call, a call destined to change forever both Abraham and the history of the world. Abraham was to leave his old way of life and step out by faith. He would be given a land of his own. He would become the father of many nations, and he would be blessed. Such was his call.

We think, too, of *the cost*. The price of obedience was high. He was to get out of his father's house and turn his back upon his kindred. His first response was a hesitant kind of half obedience. He accompanied his father as far as Haran, a frontier town of ancient Mesopotamia, devoted to the worship of the moon god; and there Abraham tarried. He made no further progress until his father died.

After the funeral he made his real move and set forth on his pilgrimage. Evidently he followed the ancient trade road across the Fertile Crescent until he came to Canaan. Then God spoke again: "Unto thy seed will I give this land," He said (Gen. 12:7). The promise was repeated later on and greatly enlarged. The land grant stretched from the Nile to the Euphrates. It was the hub of three continents and the most strategic spot on earth.

But now came *the crisis*. Abraham discovered that the foul Canaanite was entrenched in the land, his land. Pagan though he once had been, Abraham must have been appalled by the filthiness and fierceness of Canaanite religion. How was he to get rid of the Canaanite? And, just as disconcerting, the land was in the grip of a famine. It was a crisis indeed! But God invariably puts us to the test at the commencement of a new venture of faith.

Then came *the climax*. The Genesis account focuses on Canaan. The account in Hebrews 11 focuses on heaven, for that was Abraham's real goal: "He looked for a city which hath foundations, whose builder and maker is God." That great city drew him like a magnet. He was but a pilgrim and a stranger down here. The possession of the Promised Land of Canaan was a mere incident in God's great plan. This Abraham understood. Beyond Canaan, his heart and true home were over there in glory.

It should be thus with us. The Lord sets before us the vision of another country, a heavenly country. We start for that fair land the moment we are saved. Our true citizenship is up there, so we are to be strangers and pilgrims down here. Our calling is to be ambassadors to those who live down here, and to urge them to join us over there.

THE BONES OF JOSEPH

HEBREWS 11:22

Someone has said that in no less than one hundred fifty ways, Joseph is like Jesus. Certainly there are numerous ways this is so. The Holy Spirit Himself emphasizes just one of them: "By faith Joseph, when he died, made mention of the departing of the children of Israel; and gave commandment concerning his bones." The bones of Joseph are mentioned four times in the Bible.

The first time we meet these bones (Gen. 50:25), we hear them say to the Israelites: "God will bring you out." There is Joseph on his deathbed with his family all gathered around. Though Joseph was one of the great lords of the land, there was to be no state funeral. He spent no money on a costly tomb in Egypt, for he had other plans. Those who crowded around him were eager to know how he intended to leave his wealth. We can imagine their dismay and disappointment when he reads his will and says: "I bequeath you my *bones!*" Little did they know; but for some four hundred years, those bones would bear silent testimony to a nation of slaves: "God will bring you out of this land." God had promised it to Abraham. Joseph believed it. Israel forgot it. Joseph's bones confirmed it. However, it was the promise of *coming redemption*.

Joseph was offered the treasures and pleasures of Egypt. God, however, had kept him true—as a lonely lad, and as a lord of the land, in the prison and in the palace. *Adversity* could not conquer him; *advancement* could not corrupt him. All that Egypt had to offer was his to command—power, position, prosperity, pleasure, and praise. But on his deathbed, we see a man sick to death of Egypt. "God," he said, "will bring you out, out, out of this land." His bones were to remind the Hebrews that they belonged to another country.

He said, "Ye *shall* carry up my bones." He wanted to be buried in Canaan. Jacob had insisted on the same thing. One day, the day Christ arose from the dead, there would be a resurrection of saints in the Promised Land. Joseph wanted to be there when it happened.

The second time we meet the bones of Joseph (Exod. 13:19), we hear them say to the Israelites: "God will bring you through." It is the night of the Exodus. The avenging angel has passed through the land. And from the Delta to the mountains of Ethiopia, all Egypt knew that the God of the Hebrews was a God to be feared. The death of every firstborn in the land acted as a spur. They begged the Hebrews to leave and loaded them down with gifts. Everyone was carrying something of value. What do you think Moses was carrying—some special Egyptian treasure? Oh, no! Nothing like that. The Bible says that "Moses took the bones of Joseph with him." He knew their value. All the way from Egypt to Canaan that body, the body of Joseph, was a memorial body. It whispered to Moses, "God has brought you out; God will bring you through." In the great crisis experiences along the way, others trembled but Moses trusted; others were conquered by fear, but Moses was controlled by faith. He had the bones of Joseph to remind him of God's promises.

The third time we meet the bones of Joseph (Josh. 24:32), we hear them say to the Israelites: "God will bring you in." In the end, Joshua fell heir to Joseph's bones, and he buried them in Canaan. They were at rest at last. God had overcome all obstacles and every foe. The people were at rest.

But Joseph's bones still had something to say. Put your ear to his costly casket. Those bones of his think it a wonderful joke! The Hebrews thought they had got it all when they conquered Canaan, but the bones of Joseph knew better. His foot bone is talking to his anklebone; his anklebone is talking to his shinbone: "Now hear the word of the Lord!"

"Sure!" they say. "They've buried us in Canaan, but we're not going to settle down. God will surely visit us and carry up these bones from thence. He brought us here, but we are not here to stay. God will surely bring us up. For Joseph died in hope of the resurrection. And so do we."

Devotion 75

THE TEMPTATIONS OF MOSES

HEBREWS 11:24–26

Moses ranks along with Abraham, David, and Daniel as one of the truly great men of Old Testament times. His shadow looms over centuries of Hebrew history. His influence is felt in courts of justice in the Western world to this day. It all stemmed from a decision he made when he was "come to years." Satan came to him and offered him three things. First, he offered him *the throne of this world.* He had been found in his little ark of bulrushes in the reeds along the banks of the Nile by no less a person than the princess royal of Egypt. She had adopted him and taken him into the palace to be trained to rule. Moses was "learned in all the wisdom of the Egyptians," the Holy Spirit says (Acts 7:22). The arts and sciences, religion, history, the art of government, and the craft of war—Moses excelled in them all. And when he was a grown man, the throne itself appears to have been offered to him by the princess herself. The princess who adopted him was likely the vigorous and determined Hatshepsut, a strong-willed woman who seized the throne and reigned as sovereign in her own right. She was so strong a ruler she was able to keep Thutmose III, one of the most powerful empire-building pharaohs, off the throne for some twenty-two years. Doubtless Thutmose and his faction feared that Moses would supplant him.

Moses, however, was controlled by his faith in God and declined the offer. He went further. He "refused to be called the son of Pharaoh's daughter" (Heb. 11:24). Doubtless the tempter whispered: "You can use the throne to mitigate the sufferings of your fellow Hebrews in their ghetto in Goshen. You can even settle them in Canaan as allies of Egypt." Moses, however, gave up the throne of this world.

He also gave up *the thrills of this world.* He turned his back on "the pleasures of sin." There was no lust he could not have indulged. There was no sin he could not have gratified, and gratified with the sly approval of the world. He chose "rather to suffer affliction with the people of God, than to enjoy the pleasures of sin for a season" (Heb. 11:25). The Bible does not deny that there are pleasures in sin because obviously there are. The point is, they do not last and do not satisfy. They are only "for a season."

Finally, he gave up *the things of this world*. The Egyptians were very good at making things. When Howard Carter, the Egyptologist, excavated the tomb of Tutankhamen, he found himself thirty feet from the outer door, down a long tunnel he had excavated. Before him was a second door. He made an opening in that door and thrust a candle through the opening. Lord Carnavon, his sponsor, demanded, "What is it?" "I see wonderful things," Carter finally exclaimed, "wonderful things."

Things! Wonderful things! Moses gave them all up. He esteemed "the reproach of Christ greater riches than the treasures in Egypt" (Heb. 11:26). So Satan left him. And God came, crowned him with glory and honor, enriched his life, and made him a renowned emancipator and legislator, and an Old Testament saint as well. He will do the same for us if we make the kinds of choices Moses made.

SAMSON

The Hebrew Hercules

HEBREWS 11:32

He was the Hebrew Hercules, a mighty man of strength who rejoiced in his strength and loved to use it to mock the foes of the people of God. His name was Samson. His name means "shining like the sun." And that gives us a clue as to how we should view his spectacular life.

We begin with *the morning sunrise* of his life, a morning full of promise—such promise indeed as might have made him the greatest type of Christ in the entire Old Testament. Though sadly tarnished by his shortcomings and sins, flashes of his Christlikeness shine through.

At first, all was of Christ. His birth, like that of Jesus, was foretold and was a miracle birth. Samson grew up in seclusion under the blessing of God, and the Spirit of God rested upon him. Indeed, the Spirit of God is mentioned more in connection with Samson than with all the other judges combined.

Like Christ, Samson was set apart from before his birth to be wholly dedicated to God. He was to be a lifelong Nazarite. His long hair proclaimed that in his very *appearance* he could easily be recognized as God's man. His abstinence from wine meant his *appetites* were under control. He did not act from the stimulus of nature but from the empowering of the Holy Spirit. His separation from dead bodies, even those of his nearest and dearest, meant that his *affections* were on the altar. God came first.

As a type of Christ, he took a Gentile bride and loved her, weak and apt to betray him as she was. To get that bride, he came to grips with a lion and tore it to pieces and then brought sweetness out of death itself. This became a riddle (a mystery parable indeed) to the Philistines, who at last had to go to Samson's bride to learn what Samson meant.

Next comes *the meridian splendor* of his life. The joy of the Lord was his strength. The inner source of his extraordinary power was the Spirit of God. The outward sign of his consecration was his long hair.

As the Lord was rejected by the religious establishment, so it was with Samson. The elders of Israel did not value him. They saw him as a threat. They were afraid his activities would stir up their conquering Gentile overlords. So they conspired to hand him over to the Philistines. The enemy Philistines, however, were no match for him. He tore away the bonds with which he had been bound, seized the jawbone of an ass, and triumphed gloriously. Then, miraculously, water flowed from that vehicle of death, that old dead jawbone. Similarly, the cross became the despised instrument whereby the foe was conquered and the living water of the Spirit was set free to flow.

But then we see *the evening shadows* of his life. Women became more and more prominent in Samson's life—pagan, godless women. There was, for instance, the harlot at Gaza. How that liaison must have grieved the Spirit of God. Just the same, He did not depart from Samson at once but gave him a great victory. His carrying away of the gates of Gaza is a shadowy picture of Christ prevailing over the very gates of hell.

But then Delilah came, and the handwriting was on the wall for Samson. He had played the fool with women once too often. Besides, the Philistines now had the measure of their man. They realized that their men were no match for Samson. They decided to use a woman to overthrow him, one who was in their pay. Samson became infatuated with her. All she wanted was the secret of his power, and at last she wheedled it from him. That was the end. The enemy overthrew him, blinded him, bound him, and then set him to work to grind corn, women's work in the East. Then they planned a grandstand occasion to show him off in his shame.

But now comes *the gory sunset* of his life. Round and round the mill-stone went the fallen hero, the object of derision and scorn. "Howbeit," says the Holy Spirit, "the hair of his head began to grow again" (Judg. 16:22). The festive day arrived, a public holiday to gloat and triumph over the fallen giant. The Philistine temple was packed. "One more time!" Samson pleaded, "Oh, dear God, just one more time!" God granted his prayer. The Spirit came upon Samson and with one last, mighty effort, down came the temple, posts, pillars, people, and all. It was a gory sunset indeed.

But a red sunset heralds the coming of a new and better day. Mighty was Samson's triumph in death. Mighty, too, the victory in death of Jesus, the Sun of righteousness, who in His death and resurrection took captivity captive and gave gifts unto people (Eph. 4:8). Samson's gift to Israel was the dawn of a new day. For Samuel came, and the dark days of the judges were done. The Lord's gift to mankind was a new age of grace—soon to end, now, with an even brighter millennial age to come.

Devotion 77

YE ARE COME UNTO MOUNT ZION

HEBREWS 12:22

Mount Zion! That is *what* it is. The author of Hebrews puts it in stark contrast with Mount Sinai. Sinai was a place to turn blood to ice. The earth rolled and tumbled beneath Moses' feet at Sinai until even he quaked with terror before the Lord. From nowhere, yet from everywhere, had come the disembodied voice, with its dictates and demands; its warnings and its woes; its rituals, rules, and regulations. Sinai was no place to visit, much less to live.

Thankfully, we are transported in a moment to Mount Zion. The name is familiar to us from our Old Testament history books, where it is mentioned some one hundred fifty times. It is a place often identified with the earthly city of Jerusalem. The earthly Zion, however, is but a picture of the heavenly one.

During the millennial reign, this celestial city, the heavenly Jerusalem, will come down and take up its place in the sky, in a space-time dimension, immediately above the earthly Jerusalem. That is what it is. Mount Zion is a real place for real people. It is the home of the blood-bought saints of God. We call it heaven.

Think, too, of *whose* it is. It is "the city of the living God." The earthly Jerusalem was known as "the city of David" (I Kings 3:I). The heavenly Jerusalem is known as the city of God.

This is the city that captured the imagination of Abraham (Heb. 11:10). We know from the book of Genesis about the *voice* that spoke to Abraham, the voice that demanded he turn his back on Ur of the Chaldees, step out by faith, and become a pilgrim and a stranger on the earth. That voice turned Abraham's feet toward the Promised Land of Canaan. It is not until we are well into the New Testament that we learn about the *vision*. The vision turned his heart toward heaven at the same time that it turned his heart toward Canaan. "He went out," says the Holy Spirit, "for he looked for a city which hath foundations, whose builder and maker is God." Ever afterward Abraham had a new focus. This world was not his home; he was just passing through. His treasures were laid up somewhere beyond the blue.

Abraham was seventy-five when God called him out from Ur of the Chaldees. One hundred years later, God called him home—to the city of the living God. It is an *impregnable* city with towering jasper walls. It is an *immense* city, fifteen hundred miles square. It is an *imperial* city, where stands the great white throne. It is an *imperishable* city, engineered for eternity.

Finally, let us think of *where* it is. It is called "the *heavenly* Jerusalem." The word used is *epouranios*, literally "above the sky." The word conveys the thought of something very high. Psalm 75:6, Isaiah 14:13, and Job 26:7 all point toward the far and distant north. We project our line beyond the northward-pointing axis of the earth on into space beyond the polar star (which orientates the geography of earth and sky), and, lo, out there lies that city four square.

> A tent or a cottage, why should I care?
> They're building a palace for me over there;
> Though exiled from home, yet still I may sing:
> All glory to God, I'm a child of the King.[1]

---

1. Harriet E. Buell, "A Child of the King," 1877.

THINGS ANGELS DESIRE TO LOOK INTO

Part 1

1 PETER 1:11–12

Peter spoke of "things the angels desire to look into." One would have thought that they already had enough things to look into—managing and directing all God's vast empires in space! But no! Their attention has been caught, and no wonder! God the Son vacated heaven for earth; and, as soon as He came back, God the Holy Spirit did the same.

This desire among the angels is no passing whim. The word the Holy Spirit uses for "desire" means "to desire earnestly." The words "look into" suggest stooping down in order to do so. The angels thus desire to stoop down from the dizzy heights where they dwell to look into the great mysteries of our faith. There are at least five such marvels that fascinate those sinless sons of light.

First, they desired to look into *the cradle in the hay*. Imagine what a stir there was on high when word was passed around that the Son of God was going down to planet Earth to become the Son of Man. One moment heaven was ablaze with light. The next moment that light was shining on a cattle shed where a virgin was giving birth and a new star shone in the sky. Up in heaven they spread the news:

> Away in a manger, no crib for a bed,
> The little Lord Jesus laid down His sweet head;
> The stars in the sky looked down where He lay,
> The little Lord Jesus, asleep on the hay.[1]

I. "Away in a Manger," 1885 (author unknown).

This they must look into! And so they did! Down they came from the high halls of bliss and surrounded the nearby Judean hills, desiring earnestly to look into what was transpiring on the earth. And what do you think astonished them most? Nobody seemed to care. They raised their voices and awoke the slumbering echoes of the hills and plains. "Unto you is born this day in the city of David," they cried, "a Saviour, which is Christ the Lord. . . . Glory to God in the highest" (Luke 2:11, 14). And nobody cared. A few shepherds looked timidly around, but that was all.

The angels ceased their songs. They gazed in awe and wonder at the infant Christ, God's incarnate Son, their mighty Maker, reduced to the size of a human babe, wrapped in baby clothes, cradled in a manger in a cattle shed. Back they went to glory to proclaim the news on high.

Watch them as they arrive back on heaven's shore. The other angels gather around. "And what of the sons of men?" they ask. "What of Adam's race? They must be thrilled to know that their captive planet has been invaded at last, and by no less a one than our Beloved. Fallen Lucifer's doom is sure. How did sinners take the news? By now the tidings must be heard in all Judea, in Jerusalem, in Athens, and in Rome! There must be a stampede under way. Surely Herod has abdicated the throne by now. Surely Augustus must be bringing his legions to bow at His feet. The road to Bethlehem must be packed with people eager to look into these things."

"Interested? A stampede? No indeed! They couldn't care less. Indeed, there was no room for Him in the local inn, so they gave Him a cattle barn in which to be born, a cave, no less, with manure on the floor, and cobwebs, and a food trough for His bed. Strange folk, these humans. How sad! How strong is the stranglehold of sin!"

And so it was. And so it is. The Son of God has come, and only a handful seem to care.

Devotion 79

THINGS ANGELS DESIRE
TO LOOK INTO
Part 2

1 PETER 1:11-12

The angels looked into *the cradle in the hay*. That was something of consummate interest to them. That God should become a man was amazing! But that He should become a man by such a process and for such a purpose and at such a place was truly amazing!

Thirty years passed, and then we are told of the next thing that the angels desired to look into. Undoubtedly, however, no deed, no word, and no choice of His failed to capture their interest. A thousand books could have been written about those silent, hidden years. To us, the activities of those thirty years are all unknown. But the angels watched and listened in awe from the moment of His birth to the hour of His baptism at the hands of John.

Now comes the next turning point—*the conflict in the wilderness*. The angels knew about sin and Satan because the whole great "mystery of iniquity" had all begun in heaven, not on earth. Moreover, Lucifer appeared on high from time to time, summoned to appear before the throne of God to give account of his wanderings to and fro on the earth.

Some members of the angelic order of the cherubim had done sentry duty at the gate of the garden of Eden right after the fall (Gen. 3:24). They were posted there to guard the way to the Tree of Life. So the fall was a matter known on high. The interest of the angels was intensified by news that a fresh conflict was brewing. A second Man, a last Adam, was to take on fallen Lucifer, and under enormous handicaps. The Holy One would meet the Devil alone in a howling wilderness after He had fasted right down to the very door of death, to a point where His physical resources were gone and His life hung by a thread. How different that scene is from the glens and glades of Eden where the fall had taken place.

Behind Jericho, in the deep depression of the Jordan, far below the level of the sea, there arose the Mount of Temptation. A climber would find that with every step up its slopes the scene became worse. The desolation that lay all around was that of a land accursed. The mountain itself was arid and naked. It was a mount of malediction. It rose in steep slopes from a sun-scorched plain and looked down on the sluggish waters of buried Sodom's sea. The Dead Sea, they called it; and a fitting name it was.

The battle began. It climaxed in the presentation of the same three temptations, though in different guise, that had conquered Eve and then Adam—the lust of the flesh, the lust of the eye, and the pride of life. The angels kept well back. This was no conflict of theirs. There must be no intrusion by them. But how they cheered when Satan, beaten again and again, finally fled from the scene. Then, and not till then, God sent angels to visit the exhausted Conqueror.

The angels found their Lord at last, at the utter end of all endurance: physical, moral, and spiritual. He lay there alone, exhausted and weak but triumphant. Could this be? Was this He? It was. The Son of Man, victorious and crowned with glory and honor.

"Hello, Gabriel!" Surely some such word of welcome passed the Savior's lips. The unnamed angels ministered to Him, perhaps providing a drink of water from the crystal stream, or a bed, or a drawn sword to guard Him while He slept.

No doubt the other angels were full of questions when these privileged ones arrived back home. "But were there no men there to care for Him? What about His friends, His family?" "No! There was no one."

So He fought that fight alone, and He won! And Satan, skulking somewhere in some haunted hollow, knew that he had met his match at last. And he was terrified.

Devotion 80

THINGS ANGELS DESIRE TO LOOK INTO

Part 3

1 PETER 1:11–12

W e have seen the angels looking into *the cradle in the hay* and into *the conflict in the wilderness*. Now we see them desiring to look into *the cloister in Gethsemane*.

Just outside Jerusalem, on the lower slopes of Olivet and just across the Kidron, was an enclosed garden. It was a place of ancient trees. Their large twisted trunks and spreading branches, laden with fruit and foliage, formed a natural cloister, a retreat from the pressures of life. Jesus loved to go there. He could withdraw into its shadows and talk to His Father in heaven. It was called *Gethsemane*, which means "oil press." It was the last place the Lord sought out before He died. He came there to watch and weep and pray.

First, He withdrew "a stone's cast" from His three closest friends (Luke 22:41). That phrase, "a stone's cast," has an ominous ring to it. The Jews executed criminals by *stoning*. So "a stone's cast" referred to the distance of death. For Jesus, death was only a stone's cast away.

Mark, doubtless conveying Peter's words, says that Christ "began to be . . . very heavy" (Mark 14:33). The word he used means "deeply weighed down," or "depressed." Think of it! Jesus, the all-conquering Christ who was always in control of every circumstance, was *depressed!* In the upper room just a short time before, He had sung the Hebrew Hallelujah hymn. Now He groans, deeply weighed down by the thought of our sin.

Then, too, Mark tells us He was greatly "amazed" (v. 33) or "greatly astonished." The expression occurs only in Mark's gospel, and he uses it three times. He had used the word to describe the people at the foot of the Mount of Transfiguration when the Lord arrived in their midst, all aglow from His contact with heaven (9:15). He uses the word again, in connection with the appearance of the angel at the empty tomb of Christ. The word describes the reaction of the women. They were "affrighted" (16:5), or "thrown into terror." Now Mark uses the word to describe the Lord's grief in the garden. On both the other occasions (of the glow of glory that still clung to Him as He came down from the mount, and of the shining one who guarded the tomb) the word is associated with another world. The same is true here. As He gazed into the dark and dreadful cup being presented to Him, He was overwhelmed by the world of evil He must now embrace. The old hymn catches the idea:

> O Lord, what Thee tormented
> Was our sin's heavy load,
> We had the debt augmented
> Which Thou didst pay in blood.[1]

The angels desired to look into all this. For this was beyond their understanding—their Beloved so identified with all the horror and wickedness of our sin as to actually "be made sin" for us.

And so it was, as He came close to death there in Gethsemane at the thought of what lay ahead, angels came to strengthen Him. He must not die there, not there in a garden, but on a skull-shaped hill at a place called Calvary.

So the angels came. They ministered to Him and then, sadly, they went back home. And the heavenly hosts gather around again. "You say He was alone? Was there not a single one of Adam's race to wipe His brow and grip His hand?" "We saw three men not far off," the ministering angels would have replied. "They were friends of His—Peter, James, and John, He called them. But they were sound asleep."

So Peter, James, and John missed the opportunity of a lifetime to minister to Him in His need. How often, one wonders, have we missed some similar occasion to win high recognition and eternal reward.

---

1.   Bernard of Clairvaux, "O Head Once Full of Bruises," trans. Paul Gerhardt.

Devotion 81

THINGS ANGELS DESIRE TO LOOK INTO

Part 4

1 PETER 1:11–12

First, it was *the cradle in the hay*. Then, it was *the conflict in the wilderness*. Next, it was *the cloister in Gethsemane*. Now, it is *the crypt in the garden*. All these are things the angels have desired to look into. Twelve legions of warrior angels in high heaven, armed to the teeth with drawn swords in their hands, strained over the battlements of heaven, watching these things. They were waiting for just one word from Him. That was all. They watched as people lied about their Beloved in their kangaroo court, as they blindfolded Him and punched Him in the face, as they crowned Him with thorns, as they plowed His back like a farmer's field, as they proclaimed Him guiltless and then condemned Him to a felon's death, as they marched Him to a skull-shaped hill and spiked Him to a Roman tree. One word! That was all they wanted. It never came. Silently they put their swords away. Armageddon would have to wait. They stood around on high and watched Him take the scoffing and the scorn. They watched Him as He bowed His head and died.

Then came His friends. They took His torn and tattered body from the tree. Two men and a few sad women prepared His body for the tomb. Costly linens were produced and expensive ointments too. They wrapped Him around and around with bandages and fragrant spices. Then they put Him in a rich man's tomb in a garden in Jerusalem. They rolled a heavy stone in place and soldiers came and set the seal of Rome upon the sepulcher and left a guard to make sure no one tampered with that tomb.

The world spun on through space, carrying its priceless burden round and round its axis for three long, dragging, endless days and three dark, dreadful, dreary nights. That incorruptible clay lay in that crypt dug into the rocky face of a Jerusalem hill. And, on high, the angels desired to look into these things.

Then it happened! The Lord returned from deep within the underworld, and entered the tomb unseen by the guard, and reentered His body, pure, untainted, untouched by the faintest indignity of decay. He shed the grave clothes, which by now were stiff as a plaster of paris cast. He simply arose through them and then walked through the fast-sealed door and vanished.

Two of the angels came. Who were they? My guess would be Gabriel, the messenger angel, the communicator of God's will to men, and Michael, the martial angel, the commander of the armies of heaven. With ineffable disdain for the soldiers, they broke the seal and rolled back the stone—not to let Christ out, but to show that He was gone. Then they sat down and waited.

Perhaps they thought that the Lord's disciples would remember His promise that on the third day He would rise again. Surely they would come with the morning light. A few women appeared, and surely that stirred some interest. But they had come to do some more burying! A couple of men came later but did not stay. Nobody, it seemed, believed a word that Jesus had said.

The angels went back home. We can picture the other angels crowding in. "Now surely," they would say, "surely the children of Adam came flocking to the tomb!" "No!" one of the two privileged angels would say. "No! In fact, one of the women who came seemed distraught. She turned her back on me and wrung her hands over the empty tomb. I overheard her talking to our Beloved as though He were some gardener fellow, and as though He had hidden the missing body somewhere. How stubborn is their unbelief! Yet our Lord loves them. He has great plans for them, He says. These are some other things we should look into."

Devotion 82

THINGS ANGELS DESIRE TO LOOK INTO

Part 5

1 PETER 1:11–12

*T*he cradle in the hay—the angels desired to look into that. *The conflict in the wilderness, the cloister in Gethsemane, the crypt in the garden*—these, too, they desired to probe. But there was something else: *the concealment in the clouds.*

When God came down in olden times and pitched His tent among His people, He wrapped Himself with a most unusual cloud. They called it the "Shechinah," the glory cloud. It sat upon the mercy seat upon the ark in the Holy of Holies. It spread out over the tents of the tribes so that the sun might not smite them by day or the moon by night. Its presence was the visible token that God was resident. It was His banner; and beneath its far-flung canopy, the saints could rest secure. It took the appearance of a pillar of cloud by day and of a pillar of fire by night. In Ezekiel's day, it had withdrawn itself because of the apostasy of the people. It had gone back to heaven, and it had remained withdrawn throughout the remainder of the Old Testament era. Now the cloud was back, swirling and swaying above the Mount of Olives. The temple was ignored, for its veil had been rent in two. God was no longer there. But the cloud was back. As the Savior made His way up Olivet, there it was, hovering on high, awaiting its Lord.

Forty days and forty nights had come and gone since Jesus' resurrection. Now He was going home, and the cloud awaited Him. The angels, too, were taking up their places in the sky. They had come to herald His birth; now they had come to welcome Him home.

It seems likely that all one hundred twenty believers in the Lord were assembled on Olivet that day. They had marched with Him out of the city, down and across the Kidron, past the garden of Gethsemane, and on up to the top of the mount. There the assembled band of believers halted. Pentecost was on its way. The Lord was going up, and the Spirit was coming down. The Lord raised His hands in parting benediction. Then, silently and surely, He began to ascend. The astounded disciples stood there, gazing up into heaven. Two of the angels detached themselves from His honor guard to come back with one last word. "He'll be back!" they said, "in this same way as He has gone!" Then they too were gone. For here was something they did not want to miss, something well worth looking into. They rejoined the angel escort to see Him home and to watch His investiture in heaven. As Son of Man and Son of God, they saw Him sit down on the great white throne in heaven.

The angels still desire to look into these things. They are the talk of the ages up there. Yet, down here on earth, it is only with the greatest difficulty we can get anyone to listen when we talk of these things. Even those who say they love the Lord often pay but scant attention to these things. They neglect their Bibles, absent themselves from the meetings of the church, and have little interest in spreading the good news. The angels must surely look askance at all of us. To the angels, who desire earnestly to stoop down and look into these things, our indifference must seem like criminal neglect.

Devotion 83

CALLED THE SONS OF GOD

1 JOHN 3

Behold, what manner of love the Father hath bestowed upon us, that we should be called the sons of God." We can get into a family in three different ways. We can be *born* into a family, and in that case it is *life* that secures the relationship. We can be *adopted* into a family, in which case it is *law* that secures the relationship. Or we can be *married* into a family, in which case it is *love* that secures the relationship. The Christian is placed in the family of God in all three ways—blessed be God! "A threefold cord is not quickly broken" (Eccl. 4:12). The *Holy Spirit* is the one who puts us in the family of God by birth. The *Father* is the one who puts us in by adoption. The *Son* is the one who puts us in by marriage. What more could we ask than that?

Now, let us think what it means to have such love "bestowed upon us, that we should be called the sons of God" (1 John 3:1). Let us picture ourselves in heaven as the saints of all ages go marching in to where Christ sits on the right hand of the Majesty on high.

> There goes Abel, the first martyr of the faith. And here comes Enoch, the first raptured saint of all time. Now it is the turn of Abraham, "the friend of God." Isaac follows, the man who was "obedient unto death." And there goes Jacob, now truly "a prince with God"; and here comes Joseph, the most Christlike man in the Old Testament. And there is Job, of whom God said there was "none like him in the earth." And here comes Gideon, "mighty man of valor" that he was; and Samuel, last of the Old Testament judges and first of the Old Testament prophets. There goes Moses, the kinsman-redeemer of a nation; and Daniel, "a man greatly

beloved"; and John the Baptist, called by Jesus "the greatest man born of a woman . . ."

But wait! It's our turn now. As we come to the reviewing stand, the high halls of heaven ring with applause. Everyone stands. The trumpet sounds. The herald angel announces our fame. "These are *the children of God!* They are joint-heirs with Jesus Christ. They are seated with Him in the heavenlies, far above principalities and powers, thrones and dominions, and every name that is named, not only in this world but also in the world to come." Such is the manner of love the Father has bestowed upon us.

"Therefore the world knoweth us not," John adds, "because it knew him not" (v. 1).

Look at what the world did to God's beloved Son. He came down here and lived on earth for thirty-three years. He "went about doing good," Peter says (Acts 10:38). He lived His whole life in the service of our fellow race. He healed the sick and raised the dead. He made the blind to see and the deaf to hear. He cleansed lepers and cast out evil spirits. He changed water into wine and fed the hungry multitudes. He loved His enemies and died to save them. He taught the sublimest truths in the simplest of terms. He was love incarnate. And this world crucified Him.

If they knew Him not, it is no wonder they know us not, John says.

But the Father knows us! And He is on the throne. We may be despised and rejected down here, but we are assured of a tumultuous welcome when we arrive up there. Once we get over Jordan, the Promised Land awaits, along with the Father's welcoming smile and high seats in heaven itself.

Devotion 84

LOVE THE FATHER HATH BESTOWED

1 JOHN 3:1

When John wrote his first epistle, apostasy already had taken deep root in the church. The up and coming heresy was Gnosticism. It denied the truth along three lines. The Ebionites denied the deity of Christ. According to them, He was just another created being. The Docetists denied the humanity of Christ. They said He was some kind of phantom, void of physical being. They denied that He had come in the flesh. The followers of Cerinthus denied the union of the two natures of Christ, the human and the divine, prior to His baptism. An entity they called "the Christ" supposedly descended on Jesus at His baptism and abandoned Him prior to His crucifixion. It was all what J. B. Phillips calls "intellectualism or high-sounding nonsense" (Col. 2:8).[1]

If anyone knew the truth about Christ, it was John. He knew the truth, for instance, about the Lord's mother. He had been Mary's protector after the crucifixion. She had been entrusted to his care by Jesus Himself. John knew perfectly well that neither Joseph nor anyone else was the father of Jesus.

As for Jesus' deity, there was plenty of evidence for that. He had turned water into wine and fed the hungry multitudes with a little lad's lunch. He had walked upon the waves and stilled a raging storm. The world itself could not contain the books that could have been written about Him, John said (John 21:25). He had healed the sick, cleansed lepers, raised the dead, and conquered the tomb. John, now an old man, had been an eyewitness of these things. His scornful answer to Gnostic nonsense was simple, but adequate: *"I was there!"*

---

1. J. B. Phillips, *The New Testament in Modern English* (New York: Macmillan, 1958).

Jesus was God. He was man. He was both. He was God, in every sense of the word, possessed of all the attributes of deity. He was man, perfectly human with a human body and mind and emotions and will. He fell asleep in Peter's boat—that was His humanity. Moments later He commanded wind and waves to be still—that was His deity. He asked a woman at a well for a drink because He was thirsty. That was His humanity. Then He told her all about her life. That was His deity. It is impossible to say where the one ends and the other begins.

Against this background, John brought his readers back to basics: "Behold, what manner of love the Father hath bestowed upon us, that we should be called the sons of God" (I John 3:1). What manner of love indeed!

"Father!" That in itself was different. The Old Testament had revealed God as Elohim and as Jehovah, as Adonai and as God Most High, as Jehovah-jireh and as El-Shaddai. Jesus revealed Him as "Our Father which art in heaven" (Matt. 6:9).

More than a hundred years ago, a book was published titled, *Letters from Hell; or A Message from a Lost Soul.* In one letter we read:

> "Was there not something in vanished time," the lost one asks, "something called 'The Lord's Prayer,' beginning with 'Our Father . . .'? I vainly try to recall the sacred words. I set out to say the prayer but never get beyond 'Our Father.' I repeat these words fifty times but never get beyond 'Our Father.' I just remember there is a Father, but He is not my Father. And I am not His child. I keep on saying the two words. My soul is thirsting for their comfort. But I can find no drop of water to cool my tongue."[2]

What a tragedy it would be to know that God's manner of love would gladly put us in His family now and forever but to end up refusing to let Him do so. We must be willing to have Him be our Father. He invites us but never compels.

---

2.   Valdemar Adolph Thisted, *Letters from Hell; or, A Message from a Lost Soul* (Philadelphia: Universal Book and Bible House, 1906).

MICHAEL THE ARCHANGEL

JUDE 9

The heavenly host have their hierarchies. There are angels and arch-angels, there are principalities and powers (owing allegiance to Satan), there are thrones and dominions (who render homage and service to God), there are the rulers of this world's darkness, there are wicked spirits in high places, and there are the cherubim and the seraphim. Michael is an archangel. Just before the voice of divine inspiration and supernatural revelation falls silent, Jude gives us an unexpected look at one page in Michael's history. It has to do with the burial of Moses.

First, there was *the confrontation*. It appears that when Moses was buried in a remote and hidden spot on Mount Nebo, Satan suddenly turned up at the funeral. No doubt Michael recognized the enemy at once as the author of sin, the Father of Lies, the Serpent, the deceiver, the old lion, the destroyer, the angel of light, and the deluder of mankind. Michael knew him of old. He had known him when he was the anointed cherub, the choirmaster of heaven, glorious in beauty, and awesome in power. He knew him now as ruler of an empire of fallen angels and humans.

Michael is known as the archangel, the only angelic being so called. He is Israel's patron and the prince who stands on their side in the unseen world. He is Gabriel's ally in the defense of the nation of Israel from its human and satanic foes. In a coming day, Michael will throw Satan from the skies (Rev. 12). So Satan showed up at the funeral of Moses, confronted Michael and demanded that Moses' body be turned over to him.

Now comes *the contention*. In Hebrew history Moses ranks with Abraham, founder of the Hebrew racial family, and with David, founder of the Hebrew royal family. It was Moses who gave the Hebrew nation its magnificent legal code. It was Moses who emancipated the Hebrews from slavery and saved them from extinction. It was Moses who organized them into a great nation. It was Moses who gave them their vibrant and divinely ordained religion. It was Moses who brought the Hebrew people right up to the border of the Promised Land. He is mentioned by name at least seven hundred times in the Bible.

No sooner was Moses dead than the Israelites were ready to deify him, and Satan was eager to oblige. That was why he turned up on Mount Nebo, armed with enormous power. He wanted the body of Moses to be handed to him so that he could make it the center of a rival idolatrous Hebrew *religion*. Michael was no match for Lucifer, fallen though he was, so Michael wisely stood aside. "The Lord rebuke thee," Michael said. That left Lucifer face-to-face with God. And Lucifer is no match for Him.

Moreover, God wanted that body for *resurrection*. Satan backed down; and the body was buried, and the grave site was hidden and protected by God.

Then suddenly the body of Moses turned up, on a mountain in the Promised Land during the days of Jesus. It had been raised from the dead, and Moses had come back to visit the incarnate God on the Mount of Transfiguration. Banned from the Promised Land by God for losing his temper, for speaking inadvisably and smiting the rock, a disappointed Moses had climbed Mount Nebo to at least *see* the Promised Land before his death. Now God lifted the ban, and Moses, in person, in his body, appeared on the holy mount. What a triumph that was for Moses! God had kept the old warrior's body hidden away where even Satan himself could not find it. So Michael won after all. And so did Moses. And so did God!

Devotion 86

AN OPENING BENEDICTION
Part 1

REVELATION 1:4–6

The book of Revelation begins with a benediction. It speaks of all *the grace* that accrues to us and of all *the glory* that accrues to Christ. We begin with *the grace that accrues to us*. In the first place, it is grace that *endures*: "Unto him that loved us." Scholars tell us that the verb for love here is in the present tense. It should read "unto Him who *loves* us." It is *unconditional love*, as Moses, in his memoirs, made clear to Israel. "The Lord" he said, "did not set his love upon you, . . . because ye were more in number than any people; for ye were the fewest of all people: But because the Lord loved you" (Deut. 7:7–8). Why does He love us? It is simply because He loves us! It is unconditional love.

It is also *incomparable love*. During one of his crusades in England, D. L. Moody was accosted by a young man named Henry Morehouse. "If I were to come to Chicago," he said, "would you let me preach in your church?" Moody gave a half promise and then forgot about it. He did not expect that such a thing would happen.

Some while afterward, who should turn up at Mr. Moody's door but young Henry Morehouse. "Hello, Mr. Moody," he said, "I have come to preach in your church." Trapped, D. L. Moody agreed to let him preach one night. "The fellow can't do much damage in one night," he confided to his deacons. "If he says anything out of line, I'll get up and correct him."

That night Henry Morehouse preached on John 3:16. He preached on the love of God. He preached with passion and power. D. L. Moody had never heard anything like it. It moved him deeply. It changed his whole concept of preaching. Indeed, Henry Morehouse became known as "the man who moved the man who moved millions."

They asked him to preach again, and again, every night for a week.

For a whole week Henry Morehouse preached on John 3:16 and on the love of God. At the end of the week, he said, "I have been trying to tell you how much God loves you. If I could borrow Jacob's ladder and climb to the city of God and ask Gabriel, the herald angel, to tell me how much God loves the world, I know what he would say: 'God so loved the world He gave His only begotten Son.'"

Such is the grace that accrues to us. "Can anything separate us from the love of Christ?" asks Paul. "Can trouble, pain or persecution? Can lack of clothes and food, danger to life and limb, the threat of force of arms? . . . No, in all these things we win an overwhelming victory through Him who has proved his love for us. I have become absolutely convinced that neither death nor life, neither messenger of Heaven nor monarch of earth, . . . nor anything . . . in God's whole world has any power to separate us from the love of God in Jesus Christ our Lord!" (Rom. 8:35–39).[1]

"Unto him who *loves* us!" What a way to begin a book dedicated to an outpouring of God's wrath!

1.   J. B Phillips, *The New Testament in Modern English* (New York: Macmillan, 1958).

AN OPENING BENEDICTION
Part 2

REVELATION 1:4–6

In this beginning benediction, John sets before us *the grace that accrues* to us. It is grace that *endures*. The benediction is addressed to the One who loves us and who keeps on loving us. It is also grace that *emancipates*: "Unto him that . . . washed us from our sins." Some versions read "*loosed us* from our sins." Dean Alford says there is a difference of only one letter between the two readings in the original. If we read: "Unto him that . . . *washed* us from our sins," then sin is regarded as a *stain*. If we read: "Unto him that . . . *loosed* us from our sins," then sin is regarded as a *chain*. Of course, it is both.

Sin is a stain. When God wanted to teach this truth to His ancient people Israel, He had them build the tabernacle in the wilderness. At one end He sat in the Holy of Holies, a thrice-holy God, wrapped in the Shechinah glory. At the other end stood the sinner in all his guilt and need. The problem was how to bring that guilty sinner from "outside the camp" to "inside the veil." Even in the sinner's earliest, most tentative, initial steps, he was made aware that he was stained by sin.

The sinner came first to the brazen altar. The great brazen altar, just inside the gate of the tabernacle court, was there to remind the sinner of his sin and the need for a *radical* cleansing from sin. Blood had to be shed.

Once he was past the brazen altar, he came to the brazen laver. He now discovered he needed a *recurrent* cleansing from sin. He had taken but a few steps, and, and, behold, he was defiled again. He needed to be washed in water, what Paul calls "the washing of water by the word" (Eph. 5:26). Sin is indeed a stain. The blood provides our radical cleansing; the Book provides our recurrent cleansing.

But, also, *sin is a chain.* Nobody outside of the Bible has caught that truth better than Charles Dickens in his famous book, *A Christmas Carol*. He shows us old Ebenezer Scrooge, sitting alone in his dingy room one Christmas Eve, not suspecting he is about to receive a visit from the ghost of his dead partner, Jacob Marley. He is startled by the ringing of some disused bells in the far recesses of the house. "The bells ceased," writes Dickens. "They were succeeded by a clanking noise, deep down below; as if some person were dragging a heavy chain in the wine-merchant's cellar."[1]

Presently the ghost of Marley comes in through the barred and bolted door. Scrooge recognizes him at once. But the thing that rivets his attention is the chain that Marley has clasped about his middle. It is long, and it winds about him like a tail. It is made of cash boxes, keys, padlocks, ledgers, deeds, and heavy purses wrought in steel.

"You are fettered," ventures Scrooge. "I wear the chain I forged in life," replies the ghost. "I made it link by link . . . I girded it on of my own free will, and of my own free will I wore it. Is its pattern strange to you? . . . Or would you know the weight and length of the strong coil you bear yourself? It was full as heavy and as long as this, seven Christmas Eves ago. You have labored on it, since. It is a ponderous chain!"[2]

And so it is. The strong chain of evil habit holds multitudes in its iron grip.

Well, thank God, Jesus has both *washed* us and *loosed* us. As the holy hymn says,

> He breaks the power of canceled sin,
> He sets the prisoner free;
> His blood can make the foulest clean,
> His blood availed for me.[3]

---

1. Charles Dickens, *A Christmas Carol: The Original Manuscript* (1843; repr., Mineola, NY: Dover, 1971), 11–12.

2. Ibid., 13.

3. Charles Wesley, "O For a Thousand Tongues to Sing," 1739.

Devotion 88

AN OPENING BENEDICTION
Part 3

REVELATION 1:4–6

This remarkable benediction celebrates *the grace that accrues to us*. It is grace that *endures*. It is grace that *emancipates*. But it is also grace that *elevates*: "Unto him that . . . hath made us kings and priests unto God."

Notice that word "made"—He "hath *made* us." It reminds us of the Prodigal Son in Luke 15. He had two prayers. He had a going-away prayer, and he had a coming-home prayer. Here is his going-away prayer: "Father, *give* me!" It was a sinful, selfish prayer, the prayer of a young rebel tired of restraint; tired of goodness; longing for the far country with its fun, its freedom, its fraternities, and its fast women. The Prodigal saw all these anticipated joys through starry eyes, and he longed for them with eager desire. "Father, give me," he said. He needed cold cash to translate his dreams into deeds.

Here, by contrast, is his coming-home prayer: "Father, *make* me!" It was the prayer of a broken and contrite heart. We see him, broken and bankrupt, heading for home with faltering steps. He still had a long way to go when his father saw him and ran and with compassion fell on his neck and kissed him. "Make me as one of your hired servants." That was to be the son's prayer. But before ever he got to that part, the father broke in with a cry for a robe and a ring and for a fine, fatted calf for a feast. He was going to show this son of his how a father can love, and how a father can loose, and how a father can lift.

It is just so with God! His is grace that endures, grace that emancipates, and grace that elevates. "Unto him that . . . hath *made* us," cries John (Rev. 1:5–6). He has made us kings and priests unto God. That is to say, He has bestowed on us all the majesty of a prince and all the ministry of a priest. This is His offer, in the Apocalypse, to a generation living on the edge of fearful judgment. It is His offer to us and to our degenerate generation today.

The benediction closes by celebrating all *the glory that accrues to Him.* "To him be glory and dominion for ever and ever." Note, first, it is *personal* glory—"To *him* be glory."

When Queen Victoria celebrated her Diamond Jubilee, she had been on the throne of Britain for sixty years. She ruled the largest empire in history, an empire spread out over a quarter of the land mass of the world. A procession was arranged to celebrate her glory. Troops from a score of countries that owned her sway marched past her in triumph. The crowned heads of Europe came. Some forty Indian rajas marched. The world sent its delegates. But it was really *her* glory. As Mark Twain put it, "The Queen . . . was the procession herself; . . . all the rest of it was mere embroidery."[1] It is the same with Jesus. To *Him* be glory. It is His and His by right.

It is personal glory. No one else can compare with Him. But it is also *positional* glory: "To him be glory and dominion." The dominion Adam threw away in the garden of Eden has been retaken by Christ. Now all glory and all dominion belongs to Him. It will be displayed to all the world one of these days.

Finally, it is *perpetual* glory: "To Him be glory and dominion for ever and ever." It will be displayed on earth for a thousand years during the Lord's millennial reign. But people will tire of that in the end. Their unregenerate hearts will loathe His iron rule of righteousness and long for the merry old days when sin could be indulged. Satan will find them easy dupes to his final batch of lies. Even that golden millennial age will pass away. It will be replaced by a new heaven and a new earth. Vast new empires in space will be created, and glory and dominion, cheered and unchallenged, will fill all of God's endless domains forever and ever. Blessed be God! Well might we sing:

> To Him whom men despise and slight
> To Him be glory given;
> The crown is His, and His by right
> The highest place in heaven.[2]

---

1. Mark Twain, *The Complete Essays of Mark Twain,* ed. Charles Neider (Cambridge, MA: Da Capo, 2000), 199.
2. Thomas Kelly, "Behold the Lamb with Glory Crowned."

Devotion 89

THE POSTMAN FROM PATMOS AT EPHESUS

REVELATION 2:1–7

It had been a great church. Indeed, it had been Paul's best church, born in a Holy Spirit revival. The whole area, for many miles around, had felt that awakening. Churches had sprung up like mushrooms on the moor. Paul's letter to Ephesus contains the most glorious truths ever revealed to mankind. Paul, Timothy, and John had all ministered there. It had an eldership of godly men, trained and taught by Paul, forewarned and challenged by him, and charged by him to watch out for the wolves.

By the time John wrote Revelation, the wolves were already playing havoc with the flock in other parts of the world. They had not yet done much damage at Ephesus, however, thanks to its wise and watchful elders. The wolves were lurking around, snarling in the shadows, eager to move in, but anyone wanting to get into that church must first get past the elders, which was no easy task.

We can picture the postman from Patmos as he arrives at this, the first of seven sister churches on his list. At the door of the church, he is met by one of the elders. Perhaps he was one of those men who, forty years before, had met with Paul at Miletus (Acts 20). The conversation might go something like this.

"Good morning!" says the elder.

"Good morning!"

"I am Barnabas of Ephesus. Who are you?"

"Me? I'm Lucius of Rome, a courier and a Christian."

"So, you're a Christian. How were you saved?"

He gives his testimony.

"Have you been baptized?"

"Oh, yes!"

"What think ye of Christ? Where do you stand on the inerrancy of Scripture?" And so on and on it goes. The postman is given a thorough grilling before being allowed to take his place in the church. The elders were watching for the wolves. They were *standing up for the truth*.

The postman finds a seat. As he looks around, he sees some of the Nicolaitans, a group of semi-professional functionaries who wore distinctive clothing and seemed to have a monopoly of sorts on preaching and praying, a kind of embryonic clergy. The church as a whole, however, seemed to be *standing up to the test*, for so far this tendency to divide between clergy and laity was in its infancy and not too sure of itself.

But what impresses the postman most is the long list of announcements of coming church activities and events. They seem to be endless. There is something going on all the time. The church is *standing up to the task*. It is indeed a very busy church.

But now the service is over, and the benediction is read. The postman from Patmos jumps to his feet. "Excuse me, my brothers," we can hear him say. "I have just been over to Patmos. I've seen the apostle John. He has a letter for you. I'll read it. It's very brief."

The central message of the letter is to the point: "I know all about you," Jesus said. "You are a Bible-believing church, and you are a very busy church. But I have something against you. You people do not love Me anymore. And that is so serious that, unless there is a Holy Spirit revival at Ephesus, I'm going to close you down. I have no use for a church that doesn't love Me anymore."

How many of our busy, fundamentalist churches, we wonder, could stand that test, the vital test of love? Poor, insolvent Ephesus! All the coin of her spiritual commerce was revealed as worthless, counterfeit, and spurious. It never came from the royal mint of love.

Devotion 90

THE POSTMAN FROM PATMOS AT SMYRNA

REVELATION 2:8–11

The postman from Patmos might have found it difficult to discover where the church at Smyrna met. Christians were not popular in those parts, so their meeting place was not likely to be advertised. The believers witnessed, of course, but they found it prudent to keep a low profile. When the postman did succeed in finding their meeting place, he would most certainly have been required to give full proof of his integrity. He may even have had to show them John's letter and signature.

He soon sorted out the saints, however, once his credentials had been endorsed and he was shown to his seat. Over there, for instance, were some *broken* people. Indeed, there were quite a number of them, people who evidently had known the pain of persecution for they bore in their bodies the marks of suffering. And there were empty seats, too, and widows and orphans, all the usual proofs of persecution—people broken in body, if not in spirit.

Then, too, there were some *bankrupt* people. They, too, seemed to be a numerous group. They were people who had suffered the loss of all things and now lived off the charity of the church. There were Jewish believers among them, excommunicated by the synagogue and plundered of all they possessed. And there were Gentile believers whose goods and homes had been confiscated by the state for refusing to put a pinch of salt on Caesar's altar in the marketplace.

But over yonder was yet another group of people, *blasphemous* people no less. These people had espoused a strange form of heresy. They were Gentiles who had embraced Judaism but nevertheless considered themselves to be Christians. As if it were not enough for the church to be persecuted by outsiders, now it had apostasy within. The Lord described their particular circle of "fellowship" as "the synagogue of Satan." They had turned away from the truth. They were not Jews returning to the synagogue, though that would have been bad enough. These were Gentiles who had crucified to themselves the Son of God afresh and put him to an open shame (Heb. 6:4–6). They had embraced a Christ-rejecting religion, submitted to circumcision, embraced the Law as a system, elevated the Sabbath, and proclaimed themselves to be Jews. But they were not Jews. Nor were they Christians. They belonged to the synagogue of Satan, a synagogue created by Satan to snare them.

Thankfully, the postman from Patmos saw yet another group of men. They were *bold* people who were undaunted by the persecution that was already their lot in life. The Holy Spirit sums up the brief but fierce time of persecution that awaited this church as "tribulation [for] ten days." Stripes and imprisonment awaited them, but they would be faithful unto death. And for all such, the promise of the Lord was that they would receive a crown of life.

The postman must have marveled at such a collection of people. The Lord appropriately addressed this congregation as one "which was dead, and is alive." And He promised that its overcomers would not be hurt of the second death.

Most churches today have the same odd mixture of truth and error, of faith and fear, of conviction and compromise. We must be overcomers, victorious believers triumphing over foes within and without, faithful in the face of persecution, and determined one day to wear a crown.

Devotion 91

THE POSTMAN FROM
PATMOS AT PERGAMOS

REVELATION 2:12-17

A t Smyrna the postman from Patmos had discovered Satan's *syna-gogue*, right there in the church. At Pergamos he discovered Satan's *seat*. For many years now the cult of the ancient pagan mysteries, long centered at Babylon, had been housed at Pergamos. It was an important power base of the Evil One. From Pergamos he energized and directed the idolatrous worship of all the world's pagan religions.

The church had invaded the world, born of wind and flame, injected suddenly and sublimely into history at Jerusalem. Satan's goal, of course, was to retaliate. The advent of the church had taken him completely by surprise at Pentecost. Its victorious banners were springing up everywhere in the world—and the world was his domain. What he wanted to do was move the world into the church; and he would ultimately succeed, not at Pergamos, indeed, but at Rome.

For the present, however, he had to make do with persecution. He launched ten distinct onslaughts on the church, led by ten Caesars from Nero to Diocletian. The whole savage scheme failed. The day would come when he would replace all these persecuting Caesars with one persuasive, patronizing Caesar. Diocletian would be replaced by Constantine, and the world would move into the church. And Satan's seat would be moved in with it.

But all that would be later. For now, when the postman from Patmos arrived at Pergamos, he at once felt the pressure of the atmosphere. Satan's seat was somewhere in that city. Pergamos was a dark, depressing, dangerous place to be.

Once he was inside the church at Pergamos, two things became apparent to him. First were the *faithful disciples* at Pergamos. They upheld the name of the Lord Jesus. That was the secret of their power, a power Satan well understood and feared. Satan fears the name of Jesus. It is the *saving* name: "Whosoever shall call upon the name of the Lord shall be saved" (Rom. 10:13). It is the *sanctifying* name; we are to "do all in the name of the Lord Jesus" (Col. 3:17). It is the *sovereign* name, for at that name every knee will one day bow (Phil. 2:9–11). Behind that name is all the power and authority of the Godhead. And Satan is no match for God, as he very well knows.

So the faithful disciples at Pergamos held high the banner of Christ. And Satan, for his throne and all his threats and all his throngs of fallen angels and demons, could do little about it. Indeed, he could do nothing at all apart from permission from a higher throne than his. He already had tried persecution. One disciple we know of, Antipas by name, had been slain. Very likely the disciples at Pergamos would have taken the postman to the very place where the martyrdom took place. They would point out the bloodstains. They would take him to the tomb and vow their loyalty to the Lord afresh.

But there was a darker side, for there was *false doctrine* at Pergamos. The Lord bluntly called it "the doctrine of Balaam" (Rev. 2:14), and it was more deadly than fire, scaffold, and sword. Satan had succeeded in getting some of his own accepted as Christians by the unwary believers at Pergamos.

The Old Testament "doctrine of Balaam" mentioned here refers to the advice Balaam, a psychic of repute, gave to King Balak of Moab, as recorded in Numbers 24:25–25:3 and 31:16. After four futile attempts to curse God's people, a people God had blessed, Balaam said to the king: "You cannot curse them, my lord king, so I suggest that you corrupt them. You cannot conquer them with the men of Moab no matter how many or how mighty they be. So try the women of Moab." That attempt to seduce God's people had succeeded only too well.

Now Satan was trying the same old trick again. The infiltration of the church by unbelievers had begun, and infidelity started to raise its head. The result was that there were some in the church who advocated a more liberal approach to things—toleration of extramarital affairs, toleration of extrabiblical doctrines, and especially toleration of those who still had fellowship with idols. The champions of idolatry would maintain that idols were only visual aids to worship. The Lord, however, was outraged. "Repent!" He said, "or else!" If they would not act, *He* would. Already the sword had been drawn. It was repent, or else! It still is.

Devotion 92

THE POSTMAN FROM PATMOS AT THYATIRA

REVELATION 2:18–29

When the postman from Patmos arrived at the church at Thyatira, he met "that woman Jezebel," as the Holy Spirit calls her. It has been suggested that she was the wife of the pastor or the presiding elder. She certainly was the driving force and inspiring genius of the church, whoever she was.

There was, of course, an Old Testament Jezebel, a woman of pagan convictions who was the doom and downfall of her husband and the curse of Israel and Judah (I Kings 16:30–33). Her husband was putty in her hands. She mobilized the secular arm of the government to persecute the true people of God. And she promoted, with all the power of the throne, idolatry and gross immorality to replace the true faith in Israel.

The New Testament Jezebel was her counterpart in the church. The Old Testament Jezebel knew how to make herself attractive and how to turn on the charm. She was clever, persuasive, and vindictive. Her counterpart in the church at Thyatira doubtless was the same.

The postman surely took note of her *boastful title*. She called herself "a prophetess." By the time the New Testament Jezebel seized the pulpit at Thyatira, the New Testament gift of prophecy was over. John was already writing the Bible's last book. So her claim was false. She called herself a prophetess, the Holy Spirit declared. What she preached was false. Her doctrine came from Satan, not from God.

We know something about her *brazen teaching*. She openly advocated a permissive attitude toward sexual sin and encouraged a liberal attitude toward idolatry and pagan festivals. In the church of those days (as in churches in pagan lands today), both immorality and idolatry were part of many believers' backgrounds. They had "turned to God from idols" (1 Thess. 1:9). What kind of spineless or godless man was this woman's husband? No doubt he was someone as weak and willful as Ahab of old, the wishy-washy husband of the Old Testament Jezebel. And what kind of men were the other leaders of the church to put up with such teaching? Such was the fatal fascination of this woman, however, that even the Lord's servants were being seduced by her. It was not merely that this wicked woman smiled when professing believers had a lapse and fell into immorality and idolatry. She actively taught people to have fellowship with paganism and claimed prophetic authority for doing so. She was demon inspired.

Little did this woman know, however, that she was living on *borrowed time*. God was patient. He gave her time to repent. His love is such that it even embraces people like Jezebel and Judas. It never occurred to this New Testament Jezebel that the only reason God had not already acted in judgment was because He had pity for her lost soul and would rather see her repent than send retribution.

Then came the *bitter torment*. The sandglass of God's patience ran out. "I will cast her into a bed," God said (Rev. 2:22). It was to be a bed of torment, a bed of some dreadful disease, perhaps, where she would toss and turn in pain. Her punishment would be commensurate with the crime.

And her children, those who had embraced her doctrines and had become ten thousand times more the children of hell than herself, would share in her doom. But that had not yet happened when the postman passed that way. Jezebel of Thyatira doubtless would have liked to lay her hands on the letter he brought and tear it to shreds. The faithful postman saw to it that it fell into the hands of the faithful ones in the church. Not just the church local, the church at Thyatira, but the church universal would need that letter, too, when Jezebel's apostasy came to full flower at Rome.

Devotion 93

THE POSTMAN FROM PATMOS AT SARDIS

REVELATION 3:1–6

The postman from Patmos had been hearing about this church from the moment he arrived in Asia Minor. It had made a name for itself. It was a church with a *reputation*. That was the first thing of note about this church. It was known far and wide as a live church. Great must have been the disappointment of the postman, therefore, when he discovered that the church was dead. And that even what was still valid was in danger of dying as well. "Thou hast a name . . . and art dead" (Rev. 3:1). So the Savior summed up the situation at Sardis.

There are stars in space, billions of light years away, which seem to be shining brightly but in reality are actually dead. They are dark now, but their light still reaches us and will do so for ages still to come. *They are shining solely by the light of a brilliant past.* So it was at Sardis. Once it had been alive, shining brightly in its corner of the world. But no more! Now all it had was a reputation. The majority of its members were taken up with personalities, programs, and politics. Outwardly all was well. It seemed to have a viable testimony. People in faraway places talked about it enthusiastically. But it was all hollow; a reputation was all it had.

But then there was its *remnant*. They, too, had a name—"Thou hast a few *names* even in Sardis which have not defiled their garments," Jesus said (v. 4). Doubtless the postman from Patmos met some of these, but they were a despised minority in the church. The new leadership wanted to be rid of them, we can be sure. They were labeled as obscurantists, as obstructionists, as old-fashioned, as old fogies. They were a nuisance, always voting against the new policies and the new programs, always calling for a return to the Book, to the basics, and to the early beginnings.

All John's sympathies were with these. He had been there, back at the beginning, when Jesus lived on earth. He had been there when the church was born with a rush and a roar in an upper room in far-off Jerusalem. He had been there when the power of the Holy Spirit reigned supreme. All John's writings had that in mind. He, the last living charter member of the church, a survivor from the first generation, wrote with passion to this compromising third generation. John's sympathies would all be with the remnant at Sardis. Probably it had been his banishment that had made it possible for the modern majority to move in.

But there was something else at Sardis. There was a *reckoning*. The Lord issued a barely veiled threat—the dread possibility of names (we are back to names again) being blotted out.

One of two things happens to us in this life: either our sins get blotted out (Isa. 44:22), or our names get blotted out. When sins are blotted out, God remembers them no more (Heb. 8:12; 10:17). So it is when names are blotted out. The ultimate horror of a lost eternity will be to realize that God Himself no longer remembers the names of those who are there. The threat of such a horrifying doom hovers like a ghost in the background of this dire warning.

This brings us to the Lord's last word to this church with the big, empty name: "He that hath an ear, let him hear" (Rev. 1:6). This was the last call to this disappointing church, the last call to those who were all pretense.

Devotion 94

THE POSTMAN FROM
PATMOS AT PHILADELPHIA

REVELATION 3:7–13

The postman from Patmos had now visited five of the seven churches to which special letters had been sent by the Lord. It had not been altogether a joyous experience. Though the church on earth was still young, it had long since left its first love. There was failure everywhere. Thyatira had been the worst, though Sardis—big, boastful, and bankrupt—was not far behind. As the postman set his face toward Philadelphia, he must have steeled his heart for more of the same. Was it to be another deluded church, another debauched church, another dead church?

But he was in for a pleasant surprise, for the church at Philadelphia was different. It was experiencing a threefold revival. It was living proof that Christ was still building His church and the gates of hell could not prevail against it.

First, it was experiencing an *evangelical* revival. The Lord had set before this church an open door, and no one could shut it. It had rediscovered gospel truth. Though that church was weak and had but a little strength, it was making the gospel message heard at home and abroad. And undoubtedly people were being saved. The Devil was doing his best to cow the Christians and close the door; but the one who had the key of David, the King of glory Himself, was the one who closed and opened doors, not Satan.

He is the key to every situation. The more the Devil tries to slam doors the Lord has opened, the more he jams his fingers.

Then, too, there was an *ecclesiastical* revival. The background of this revival was the confrontation with the "synagogue of Satan." What had been conceded by the church at Smyrna was confronted by the church at Philadelphia. The believers at Philadelphia had rediscovered church truth. The "synagogue of Satan" was made up of people who confused Judaism with Christianity. They did not rightly divide the Word of Truth. The church is not spiritual Israel. Christianity and Judaism are incompatible. Christ is the end of the Law for righteousness. For Gentiles in the church to say they were Jews was a violation of truth. They had forgotten Paul's letter to the Ephesians, a circular letter well known in Asia Minor and no doubt read and copied and kept by all the churches of Roman Asia. The letter dealt specifically with the mystery of the church, an entity quite distinct from the nation of Israel. The Philadelphia believers took up the challenge, and with what little strength they had, they confronted the synagogue of Satan. The Lord promised them victory.

Finally, there was an *eschatological* revival. The church had rediscovered truth concerning the second coming of Christ. They had rediscovered the blessed hope of the church, the truth that the Lord's coming would be pretribulational. The promise was clear: "I will keep thee from the hour of temptation, which shall come upon all the world" (Rev. 3:10). The Lord was not referring to some local trial or to some persecution confined to the Roman world. The reference is to the great tribulation mentioned frequently in Scripture (Matt. 24:20–22). Along with the rediscovery of this blessed hope that the true church would escape the great tribulation was a fresh understanding of the judgment seat of Christ. "[Let] no man take thy crown," the believers are warned (Rev. 3:11).

The church was small. Its strength was small. But mighty was its recovery of fundamental truth. The postman must have left for Laodicea with a fresh spring in his step and a fresh song in his soul.

Devotion 95

THE POSTMAN FROM PATMOS AT LAODICEA

REVELATION 3:14–22

The postman from Patmos had no trouble at all, we can be sure, in finding the church of the Laodiceans. Everybody who was anybody either went there or had friends or relatives who did.

In the first place, it was *wealthy*. The Bible says it was "rich, and increased with goods, and [had] need of nothing" (Rev. 3:17). It had by far the best paying pulpit in the province. Money was never a problem at Laodicea. It had money enough and to spare. Consequently, it felt it did not need the Holy Spirit. It could buy talent just as it could buy anything else. It could buy buildings and beautiful furniture. Like the rich fool of the Lord's parable, who planned on building bigger and better barns, the church at Laodicea was rich and increased in goods. It went in for bigger and better buildings. It did not realize that its balance sheet in heaven, like that of the rich fool, was marked "Bankrupt!" "The church of the Laodiceans" (note how the Lord addresses it) was a well-run, superbly managed business—and it was a big business, too. So it could buy talent—the most polished and eloquent preacher in the province, the most talented and accomplished choir members, the most efficient and organized staff, the most professional counselors and pastors, and the most enticing programs. It was rich. It had need of nothing.

And it was *worldly*. It was a society church. The upper crust of the city had their membership there. Politicians went there for votes. Corporate executives went there to make contacts. Intellectuals went there to debate. Nobody had to be saved or baptized or believe anything in particular to belong. The most sought after commendation for membership was to be somebody in society.

It was *warned*. The Lord was not impressed by the wealthy and worldly wisdom of this church. It was *lukewarm*—that was His own word for it. It was neither hot nor cold, neither one thing nor the other, neither Christian nor pagan. Lukewarmness is the condition of a liquid when it is reduced to room temperature. Put two containers on a table, one containing boiling hot water and the other containing freezing cold water. In time, both will settle their differences by becoming conformed to room temperature. Such was the church of Laodicea. It had so accommodated itself to the temperature of the world that the Lord said it made Him sick. The church of the Laodiceans was "wretched, and miserable, and poor, and blind, and naked," He declared (v. 17). Worse! It didn't know it.

The Laodicean church reminds us of the emperor and his new clothes in the children's story. Some itinerant tailors, you remember, had offered to make him a wardrobe of invisible clothes. When he went out in his new, invisible garments, everyone else could see he was naked; but he imagined himself to be gloriously arrayed in invisible finery. Such was the church of the Laodiceans. It strutted proudly on the world stage. The watching angels saw that it was naked.

Finally, it was *wicked*. The Lord wanted no part of it. He was outside the whole thing. He had nothing to say to it or its leaders. He addressed His appeal to individuals here and there: "Behold, I stand at the door, and knock," He said. "If any man hear my voice, and open the door, I will come in to him, and will sup with him, and he with me" (v. 20). The postman delivered his letter and went on his way.

The last thing he saw as he walked on out of history was the Lord of glory shut out of His own church.

A SCENE IN GLORY

Part 1

REVELATION 4–5

Most of what we know about heaven comes from the book of Revelation. The scenes in the book alternate between heaven and earth. A scene on earth is followed by a scene in heaven. A scene in heaven is followed by a scene on earth. It is as though John, choking on the miasmas of a putrid planet, is constantly invited by God to come up to heaven for a breath of fresh air.

The throne of God is mentioned seventeen times in these two short chapters. God wants John to know that no matter what happens on earth, *He* is still on the throne. In chapter 4 the throne is a throne of *government*. In chapter 5 it is a throne of *grace*. In chapter 4 Jesus is worshiped as the *Lord of creation*. In chapter 5 He is worshiped as the *Lamb of Calvary*. In chapter 4 the inhabitants sing: "Thou are worthy . . . for thou hast created." He is worshiped as the *Author of creation*. In chapter 5 they sing: "Thou art worthy . . . for thou wast slain." He is worshiped as the *Author of redemption*.

John comes away from this encounter with heaven with a threefold remembrance. He carries with him the memory of an unforgettable *throne*, the memory of an unforgettable *throng*, and the memory of an unforgettable *thrill*, the thrill of seeing the Lord Jesus step into the spotlight of eternity and become the center of everything.

We begin with *the unforgettable throne*. We note at once there is a *mystery* connected with that throne. For instance, look at the rainbow. Unlike earthly rainbows with which we are so familiar, this heavenly rainbow is emerald in color and completely circular. And who are the mysterious living creatures, or "beasts"? And who are the four and twenty elders? Even more astonishing, God is described as a stone! We are accustomed to His being likened to various mundane things—to a shepherd, for instance, or to a human father—but not to a *stone!* These mysterious things remind us that there are aspects of God's rule that we shall never comprehend down here.

Just the same, the fact that God is likened to a jasper and to a sardius stone should not surprise us. These were the first and last stones in the high priest's breastplate. This echo from the Old Testament, and its reminder of the high priest of Israel and his ministry of intercession, draws our attention to the tender mercies and loving-kindness of our God. We learn that no matter how severe the judgments that follow, God is too loving to be unkind and too wise to make any mistakes, for the high priest of old wore the breastplate with the jasper and sardius stones on his *heart.*

God, in mercy and loving-kindness, has already lengthened the day of grace for two thousand years. Now, beginning a book that deals primarily with judgment, judgment that can be postponed no longer, God still delays. He writes chapter after chapter, revealing Himself to us in this way and in that, putting off, for yet another paragraph or two, the dreadful business now at hand. This is so much like God! He is God of might and miracle, of course; but, above all, He is a God of mercy.

Devotion 97

A Scene in Glory
Part 2

REVELATION 4–5

There is a *mystery* connected with the throne, as it looms up before us in Revelation 4. There is a *majesty* connected with it too. John details seven things about it. They give us glimpses of just what the judgment will be like that emanates from that throne of mystery and majesty.

First, it will be *flawless judgment*. The throne of God, as seen by John, was wrapped around with a rainbow. It described a perfect circle, a circle, of course, being recognized as an emblem of perfection. There will be no mistakes, no miscarriage of judgment, and no grounds for appeal. It will be flawless judgment.

It is emerald in color, the color of earth, for the coming judgment has to do with the earth. Then, too, the fact that it is a *rainbow* that encircles the throne also points us back to earth. In the Bible the rainbow is associated with the judgment of the flood. When it bursts in all its fury on the earth, then God's judgment will be flawless and related to His covenant with the earth.

Second, it will be *formal judgment*. Twenty-four thrones surround the throne of God. The elders seated on these thrones are the crowned royalties of heaven, creatures of high rank in God's government of the universe. They form a celestial jury. Their role, however, is not to decide the question of guilt. That is all too evident. These watching elders have no need to weigh evidence. The handwriting of God is already etched on the consciences of all. Guilt is already established beyond all question. The function of these elders is to declare their approval of God's decisions. The elders add another touch of formality and dignity to the court.

Third, it will be *fearful judgment*. Thunderings shake the precincts of the court. Dreadful lightning strikes terror into the hearts of those arraigned. As Moses on Sinai, surrounded by similar manifestations of God's holiness and power, did "exceedingly fear and quake" (Heb. 12:21), so those summoned here will be gripped by terror. They will tremble in mortal fear.

Fourth, it will be *factual judgment.* John saw the Holy Spirit there in all His plenitude. He is described in the plural under the title, "the seven Spirits of God" (Rev. 4:5), possibly a reference to His attributes described in Isaiah 11:2. He is now in court as Prosecutor of the entire human race. He is there to convict people of sin, of righteousness, and of judgment. He knows every thought, every word, and every deed of every man, woman, and child. He knows the time, the place, the occasion, the motive, and the consequences. In *this* life, God offers people a fair trial or a free pardon. If it is a fair trial they choose, that is what they will get. It will send them to a lost eternity.

Fifth, it will be *fundamental judgment.* The cherubim are there. In Genesis 3 they are associated with God's *creatorial* rights, and they come to guard the gate of Eden. In Exodus they are associated with God's *redemptive* rights; they overshadow the mercy seat with their wings. They are the executives of His government and His grace. Here now in heaven, actively responding to God's acts of judgment, they watch to ensure that all His rights are upheld and owned.

Sixth, it will be *final judgment.* John saw a sea of glass. The sea is the very symbol of restless change. A sea of *glass* suggests that everything is now permanent and beyond all change. It is too late for the kind of repentance that won reprieve for Nineveh in the days of Jonah. People have sinned away the day of grace. Nothing can now be changed. There is no court of appeal. This is the ultimate supreme court of the universe. What people have sown, they now must reap.

Finally, it will be *fatal judgment.* The terrifying thing in all this is that there is *no lamb* in chapter 4, no lamb at all. It was this very thing that haunted Isaac on his way to Mount Moriah (Gen. 22). He saw the knife, which spoke of death; and he saw the fire, which spoke of that which comes after death. But where was the lamb? To be brought before *this* throne, and this court, without the Lamb will be fatal indeed.

Such, then, is the majesty of the throne before which all those who have no Lamb will one day appear. How we can thank God for the Lamb of God who takes away the guilt and stain of all our sin (John 1:29)?

Devotion 98

A Scene in Glory
Part 3

REVELATION 4–5

S o, then, John comes away from the glory land with the memory of
an unforgettable *throne*. He also comes away with the memory of an
unforgettable *throng*.

The cherubim are there. The elders are there, countless angels are
there, and the redeemed are there. He draws our attention to the cherubim. They acknowledge the One upon the throne as *the holiest one* in the
universe.

John draws our attention to *the singleness of their function*: "They rest not
day and night, saying, Holy, holy, holy, Lord God Almighty, which was,
and is, and is to come" (Rev. 4:8). They acknowledge Him as Jehovah,
the one who transcends time.

The cherubim appear to be the highest of all created beings. Lucifer
was "the anointed cherub" (Ezek. 28:14) before he fell, a high-ranked
member of their order. The cherubim John saw summon up the vast
resources of their giant intellects, the fathomless depths of their emotions, and the ceaseless drive and force of their volitional powers, and
they *worship*. Worship is the one, great, supreme, overriding activity of
heaven. These sinless sons of light see the acts of God Most High. They
weigh His words and ways, and their instinctive response is to worship.
"Holy! Holy! Holy!" they cry. "He was! He is! He is to come!" "Holy!
Holy! Holy!" Elsewhere we learn that God is love. Here we learn that
God is holy. Thoughts of God's *love* melt the hearts of His friends in ten-
derness. Thoughts of God's *holiness* melt the hearts of His foes in terror.

So, then, we note the singleness of their function as they stand before
His throne. John also draws our attention to *the singularity of their form*.
One looked like a lion, one like a calf, one like a man, and one like a
flying eagle.

The first had the face of a *lion*. When *Matthew* took it in hand to give us a picture of Christ, that is exactly what he portrayed, a *lion*. The Lord Jesus was the Lion of the tribe of Judah, royal and rightful heir to David's throne.

Mark, by contrast, portrayed an ox. On one side of that ox was a plow, and on the other side was an altar. Like a banner over all was the proclamation, "Ready for either." Mark shows Christ as the one willing to give His life in service and willing to give His life in sacrifice.

Luke had yet another portrait. He showed us a man, one perfect in His humanity, peerless in His holiness, and prodigal in His helpfulness.

John, by contrast, draws the picture of a flying eagle. He shows us the One who came down from above, whose true home was up yonder, beyond the blue, in highest heaven.

Such was Jesus. He was like a lion, like an ox, like a man, and like an eagle. Such, too, were the cherubim. As they gazed upon the Lord in glory, each one took on something of His likeness. One was like a lion, one was like an ox, one was like a man, and one was like an eagle. Not even a cherub could take on all His likeness, but each one reflected something of it just the same.

The more time we spend with Jesus, the more we get to look like Him. Moses, for instance, came down from the mount with his face aglow. Stephen's face shone like an angel's. A glance will save. As the old hymn says, "There is life for a look at the crucified One"[1] (John 3:14–15; Num. 21:9); it is the gaze, however, that sanctifies. "We all," says Paul, "with open face beholding as in a glass the glory of the Lord, are changed into the same image from glory to glory, even as by the Spirit of the Lord" (2 Cor. 3:18).

---

1.   A. M. Hull, "There Is Life for a Look," 1860.

Devotion 99

THE UNFORGETTABLE THRILL

REVELATION 5

John was caught up to heaven and saw an unforgettable *throng!* He also saw an unforgettable *throne!* Now he experiences an unforgettable *thrill.* The Lamb of God is about to be placed in the spotlight of eternity, now and forever more.

First, the *challenge of God is proclaimed throughout the universe.* John saw a scroll in the hand of the One who sat upon the throne. It was the title deed of earth. "Who is worthy to take the scroll?" That was the question. "Who is fit to govern the globe?" No one! That was the answer. The question was not, "Who is willing?" for, in that case, there would have been a stampede. The question was, "Who is worthy?" A deep silence stole across the universe. Then that silence was shattered by a sob. "I wept much," said John (Rev. 5:4). He wept for the shame of it, that no one of Adam's ruined race was good enough or great enough to take that title deed and rule the world.

Then the *Christ of God is presented throughout the universe.* One of the elders could stand it no longer. Tears enough are known on earth, but there can be no tears in heaven. "Weep not," the elder said, "behold, the Lion of the tribe of Judah ... hath prevailed to open the [scroll]" (v. 5). John turned to see this Lion. Instead, He saw the *Lamb,* right there where he had been looking all along! The Lamb stood there in the midst of the elders, the cherubim, and the throne, right where He belonged—"in the midst." John had been so taken up with the sights and sounds of heaven that he missed the Lamb.

Jesus is called the Lamb only twice in the Old Testament, only twice in the Gospels, only once in the book of Acts, and only once in the Epistles. But He is called the Lamb no less than twenty-eight times in the book of Revelation.

Moreover, the word for "Lamb," here, literally means "a little lamb."

In the book of Revelation, Satan appears as a great red dragon and the Antichrist as a wild beast with seven heads and ten horns. They mobilize the massed might of the world against God and His own. All God needs in response is a little Lamb! But this is no ordinary lamb. This Lamb has seven horns, suggesting His omnipotence, and seven eyes, symbolizing His omniscience. It is the Lamb of Calvary! He comes and takes the scroll, for while He is truly God, He is yet a Son, a child of Adam's race. Moreover He is a sinless one. He is fit to rule the world. From now on all judgment is delivered to the Son.

Now the *choice of God is praised*. All heaven breaks into the Hallelujah Chorus! And all hell is forced to bring to Him its own answering tribute of praise. The Lamb is praised first at the *focal center* of things. "They sung a new song," we read, right there in glory. "Thou art worthy . . . for thou wast slain," they say (v. 9). As the old hymn puts it:

> And when, in scenes of glory,
> I sing the new, new song,
> 'Twill be the old, old story
> That I have loved so long.[1]

Ten thousand times ten thousand voices will be raised in heaven, and the universe will echo back the sounds of praise.

Then, too, the Lamb will be praised at the *furthest circumference* of things. Fallen angels and demons; principalities, powers, rulers of this world's darkness; wicked spirits in high places; along with fallen, God-hating people and even Satan himself—all will be forced to join the chorus: "Blessing, and honour, and glory, and power, be unto him that sitteth upon the throne, and unto the Lamb for ever and ever" (v. 13).

Blessed be God our God!

---

1.   A. Katherine Hankey, "I Love to Tell the Story," 1866.